BUILT BY
NOBLES OF GIRVAN

BUILT BY
NOBLES OF GIRVAN

SAM HENDERSON AND PETER DRUMMOND

The
History
Press

Frontispiece: The man who started it all: Alexander Noble himself. (Courtesy Peter Brady)

What would you expect to find on the front of something built by Nobles of Girvan? Nobles' thistle emblem, of course, in this case as seen on the bow of *Radiance*. (Courtesy Michael Craine)

First published 2010

The History Press
The Mill, Brimscombe Port
Stroud, Gloucestershire, GL5 2QG
www.thehistorypress.co.uk

British Library Cataloguing in Publication Data.
A catalogue record for this book is available from the British Library.

ISBN 978 0 7524 5451 1

Typesetting and origination by The History Press
Printed in Great Britain

CONTENTS

ACKNOWLEDGEMENTS

Fishing vessels around 50ft in length and below have a tendency to go about their work largely unremarked and unreported, something which makes it all the more challenging if one seeks to write a book recording their histories. It follows that the authors are even more than usually indebted to their 'crew' of helpers who made this book possible.

First and foremost, we record our gratitude to Alexander Noble & Sons Ltd, Girvan, and the past and present staff of that company, especially James, Peter and Alastair Noble, for assistance given with the preparation of this book, ranging from some wonderful memories of the yard and its vessels to access to the yard's historic photographs and permission to reproduce them. Most of these pictures were taken by the late John Murray in a time long before the digital age and indeed well before the age of widespread use of the 35mm camera. We wish to acknowledge the skill of Mr Murray in creating such a fine visual history of the boats built by Nobles and the co-operation of his widow, Mrs May Murray, in allowing the pictures to be used.

We record our thanks to the photographers who helped us fill in any gaps which we found in the yard's pictures and to record the appearance of its vessels in their later years. In this regard we were assisted by Michael Craine, David Linkie, James A. Pottinger, Gloria Wilson and John M. Addison. We also acknowledge much assistance with photographs given to us by William & Dianne Strachan of Studio Nova in Peterhead.

In sourcing more photographs and in researching the book we received much assistance from the late Jim Tarvit and the staff of The Scottish Fisheries Museum, Anstruther; Tim Oliver and the staff of *Fishing News*, London; Bob McCutcheon, Donald Gibson, Lenny McLaughlin, Andy Anderson, Joe Reid, Robert Gillies, Robert Ross, Kenny Gibson, Peter Maclean, the late Grieve Gemmell, the late Willie Anderson, Donald McLeod, Michael MacKinnon, Ian Gibson, Willie Jackson, Neil Jackson, Donald John McDonald, Jackie Johnston, the late Matt Sloan, David Smith, Robert George, George Forman, Neil Wilson, Lachie Paterson, Peter Kellett, Jamie Fairnie, Malcolm Townsley, Alastair Parker, Neil MacAlister, Robert Stephen, Bill Tudhope, Stuart Emery, Edward Sinclair, Mrs E. McIlwraith, Harry Henderson, Iain McIver, Jeanie Maxwell and The Scottish Marine Biological Association, Millport.

INTRODUCTION

The Girvan boatyard of Alexander Noble & Sons Ltd was founded by Alexander Noble, a native of Fraserburgh on the Scottish east coast. Alexander Noble learned the boat-building trade in Fraserburgh before becoming manager of a boatyard in Killybegs, Ireland, in 1933. He returned to Scotland in 1937 and worked with James A. Silver, yacht builders, Rosneath, on the Firth of Clyde. Amongst other activities, this yard carried out repair and maintenance work on ring net fishing vessels, including a number from the Girvan area.

Mr Noble's son, Peter, believes the concept of a boat-building and repair yard at Girvan originated from a conversation among his father and ring net skippers Willie McKenzie of *Incentive* (BA18) and Sandy Forbes of *Betty II* (BA246) at Rosneath during the Second World War. The skippers asked Alexander Noble what he planned to do after the war and mentioned that there was no boat repairing facility at Girvan. This planted in Mr Noble's mind the germ of an idea that would grow into his own boat-building company. The idea turned into reality in March 1946 when, in partnership with his son, James, he acquired a green field site on the bank of the River Girvan, just upstream from Girvan Harbour. This site, upon which boats were built in the open, was to grow into the boatyard of Alexander Noble & Sons Ltd, commonly known as Nobles of Girvan.

The first order won by the new yard was a result of an approach by the builders to the skipper instead of the other way round which would have been more normal. On learning that local skipper Peter Stephen was contemplating building a new boat, Alexander Noble visited Skipper Stephen and successfully overcame the skipper's preference for dealing with an established builder. The first keel, that of the 40ft *Margaret Stephen* (BA251), was laid in June 1946. The vessel was, at her skipper's request, planked with Columbian pine. Peter Stephen had seen this timber used for boat building in the United States and been very impressed by its quality. The hull above the water line was not painted but varnished in the traditional fashion of Scottish west-coast fishing vessels, especially ring netters.

Margaret Stephen was delivered in February 1947. In the absence of a slipway, her launch was achieved by laying planks on the soft ground and lying the boat on her bilge on a series of rollers. The power to move the vessel was provided by the muscles of a large assembly of Girvan fishermen hauling on a block and tackle assembly. The system might not have been sophisticated but it worked perfectly well and the yard's first delivery slid obediently into the water.

Margaret Stephen proved to be a fine little sea boat. She was built for seine net and clam fishing, though Skipper Stephen also used her for line fishing and spent a small amount of time fishing for herring with trammel nets on the Ballantrae Banks. When seine net fishing, *Margaret Stephen* worked as an anchor seiner in the fashion adopted by Danish fishermen, meaning she anchored the dahn buoy on one end of her seine rope while she shot her net and the remainder of the rope. Scots seiners were more commonly flydraggers, letting their seine nets drift with the tide instead of anchoring the dahn buoy, but *Margaret Stephen*'s little 36hp Gleniffer engine proved to have insufficient power for flydragging seining. Peter Stephen later had her re-engined with a second-hand 72hp Gleniffer engine originally installed aboard the MacBrayne ferry *Marquis of Breadalbane*, which worked between Largs and Millport.

Later in *Margaret Stephen*'s career her hull was painted green and the reason for this is of some interest. When the boat was back at her builders to have a damaged plank replaced, her skipper noticed that the new plank which had been fitted stood around a quarter of an inch out from the hull. At first he was extremely upset about this, but Peter Noble (who had joined the family business in 1947) explained that the new plank would be planed down so it did not stand proud and spoil the appearance of the boat. Skipper Stephen was astonished to learn that the constant scraping down of the boat for re-varnishing had, in places removed nearly quarter of an inch from the thickness of her planking. After receiving this warning of what could happen if crewmen were over-exuberant when scraping the hull and too hard on the wood, Peter Stephen decided that thereafter the whole hull would be painted.

Margaret Stephen was what fishermen called a '40-footer', though strictly speaking, that was a misnomer. She and many similar vessels in the Scottish inshore fleet were not 40ft (12.19m) in overall length but instead had overall lengths fractionally below 40ft, commonly 39ft 9in. Vessels below 40ft in overall length were allowed to seine net for white fish within the 3-mile coastal limit. This encouraged a number of fishermen to reduce the size of their vessels to just under the 40ft limit.

As the 1950s wore on, increasing numbers of Scottish inshore vessels adopted trawling for prawns and 40-footers adapted readily to this form of fishing. They adapted equally well to trawling for queen scallops and a substantial number of these boats were built for the Scottish fleet, including twenty from Nobles' yard. Nobles' second 40-footer and the second delivery from the yard, *Selina II* (BA333), was the first boat built by Nobles to feature the thistle emblem on the bow which became the yard's trademark. All subsequent fishing vessels and also some of the non-fishing boats that came from the yard carried this totem, save for a handful of boats whose owners preferred not to have their vessels so adorned.

Early days in Girvan. Two of Nobles 40-footers, *Annabelle* (BA115) and *Margaret Stephen* (BA251) are lying together on the right of the picture. (Courtesy Scottish Fisheries Museum, Anstruther)

Generally, skippers who built 40ft boats were moving away from the traditional ring net herring fishing. It was, however, possible for boats as small as 40ft to successfully fish with the ring net. Nobles' *Spes Bona* (BA17) and *Marigold* (BA16), delivered in October 1955 and January 1956 respectively, proved to be perfectly capable of success-ful ring net operation and scored a spectacular success when working together at the ringing off the point of Holy Island, Firth of Clyde, in July 1958. *Spes Bona* shot her net first and took a single ring of 400 baskets of mackerel. *Marigold* then shot her net and the two boats took another big haul. Another 400 baskets of fish were loaded aboard *Marigold* and an additional sixteen baskets of mackerel that had been meshed in her net were later picked out of the net when it was cleaned. A combined landing of over 800 baskets of mackerel was a remarkable catch for a pair of 40-footers and gave the crews a wage of £40 per man. This was big money at the time and very welcome after a lean spell of five/six weeks during which the crewmen had received no pay at all.

The big mackerel catch was by no means the only time that the two little boats were filled at the ring net. On occasion they fished to capacity at the herring in the Firth of Clyde and also at the sprats in the Clyde sea lochs, commonly Loch Goil or Loch Long or the Gareloch. Donald Gibson of *Spes Bona* remembers one occasion when both boats were filled with 380 or 390 baskets of herring in Loch Striven, though this was the result of seven or eight rings throughout the daylight hours rather than one or two spectacularly big rings.

Spes Bona and *Marigold* were not the only Nobles-built 40-footers to go to ring-ing. *Dalriada* (TT77) and *Caledonia* (TT17) were also regulars at the ring net. *Janet Lang* (CN84) and *Jessie* (CN194) were another pair of Nobles' 40-footers which ring netted together and *Annabelle* (BA115) also spent some time ringing.

Dalriada and *Caledonia* were built as multi-purpose ringer/seiners. They did well at the seine net and *Dalriada* had a haul of no less than ninety boxes of haddock while seining of Pirnmill, Isle of Arran, in 1956/57. Nevertheless, the skippers preferred pelagic fishing and tried to spend as much time as possible at the herring, even when there were good returns to be had from the white fish. While the two boats were similar, *Dalriada* was a better carrier with capacity for 90 crans of herring compared to a maximum load of 80 crans for *Caledonia*.

While *Dalriada* and *Caledonia* spent years together, they did not partner each other exclusively. Around 1960, *Dalriada* had a spell at the ring net with the Campbeltown-based *Boy Danny* (CN142). *Boy Danny* was a 53ft (16.15m) ringer built by Millers of St Monance in 1948 with capacity for 150 crans of herring. The pair put *Boy Danny*'s extra carrying capacity to good use during a remarkable seven day period when the herring started to move after lying deep for a couple of months. On the Tuesday night, the boats were filled in Kilbrannan Sound. On the Wednesday, Thursday and Friday and also the following Monday they were filled between Ardlamont Point and Tarbert. In this period the pair were regularly taking 400/600 baskets per ring.

Dalriada also fished in company with two of Weatherhead & Blackie's ringers, the 58ft (17.68m) *Catherine Anne* (TT31) and the 56ft (17.1m) *Maryeared* (TT57). In 1974, while fishing as part of this team, *Dalriada* took the last ring net catch of her-ring by a boat fishing out of Tarbert. This was a 150-basket ring taken off Ardlamont Point, which was brailed aboard *Maryeared* and grossed £1,500.

When spratting with ring nets, *Dalriada* and *Caledonia* usually worked in Loch Striven or Loch Long and landed at Greenock where their catches were bought by McMillans of Stranraer. They did well at the sprats and were often filled to capacity four nights a week. The pair also went to the sprat fishing in the Beauly Firth, though when spratting from Inverness they usually fished with pair trawls. Their first trip to the Beauly Firth was, however, not for sprats but to take part in the Kessock herring fishery with ring nets.

In 1966, *Dalriada* and *Caledonia* had been fishing on the Ballantrae Banks when the skippers heard of big fishings of herring in the Beauly Firth, just up the firth from Inverness. They headed north in the company of another 40ft ringer, the Tarbert-built *Nancy Glen* (TT10). They found over 100 boats working in the Firth, fishing huge shoals of herring. The fish were present in such vast numbers that *Dalriada*'s propeller was visibly killing them as she steamed through the water and the sheer masses of herring were such as to force some of the shoals into the Caledonian Canal lock at Inverness. Much of the fishing took place in only four fathoms of water, which suited the ringers admirably. The team's first attempt to catch Kessock herring produced 150 crans of fish that gave all three boats their quota for the night.

The boats returned to the Kessock fishing in later years but they were usually targeting sprats and not herring. The Kessock herring fishing largely died out as the sixties wore on but the spratting provided a good fishery for several years. In 1967, *Dalriada* went north with *Catherine Ann* and *Maryeared*. *Dalriada* did have her ring net aboard but seldom used it as it was easier to fish the sprats with pair trawls. *Caledonia* trawled for Kessock sprats with *Nancy Glen* and she also had a spell partnering *Sunbeam* (BCK165, later TT117). *Sunbeam* was built by the other Nobles: James Noble (Fraserburgh) Ltd. She was a 52-footer, bought second-hand by Robert Ross of *Dalriada* in 1974 when he decided to invest in a larger vessel.

Most of Nobles' 40-footers were built prior to 1960, but at the end of the sixties and the beginning of the seventies, the yard delivered a new generation of heftier and more powerful 40ft boats. *Wanderer* (BA298), *Hercules II* (BA7) and *Seeker* (CN49) were versatile little vessels, designed essentially as combination seiner/trawlers, though *Seeker* was delivered with a combined seine/trawl winch and Beccles rope coiler forward and a ring net winch in front of her wheelhouse. Her sides midships were sheathed for scallop dredging so she was actually a seiner/trawler/ringer/dredger. In her early days *Seeker* did spend some time at the ring net. Later in her career as *Sweet Promise* (SS95) she added more forms of fishing to her record of versatility, engaging in mid-water trawling and gill netting.

The new generation of 40-footers were also more powerful than their predecessors, with 112hp engines compared to the 66hp or less which had been normal on the older boats. *Wanderer* was the first Scots boat to be fitted with a tripod mast to create more space on the foredeck for her seine/trawl winch and might be the most successful of all of Nobles' 40-footers. She fished well both when seining and when single boat trawling for prawns and white fish. When catching prawns, *Wanderer* regularly out fished other 40ft boats and quite a number of larger vessels as well. Her extra engine power allowed her to tow faster and cover more ground than the older vessels and Kenny Gibson, who sailed aboard her, remembers her being a major step forward from the 40-footers which had been built at the end of the forties and the start of the fifties.

When seine netting, *Wanderer* proved herself perfectly capable of working alongside a fleet of larger seiners between 55 and 70ft long, most of which belonged to the north-east of Scotland and which came to the Clyde for the hake fishing season. Little *Wanderer* could take catches of up to 100 boxes of fish for a two-day trip. Around eighty boxes of that could be high value hake. With her expenses being much lower than the bigger boats, she was operating very profitably indeed. *Wanderer* also had a very successful spell mid-water pair trawling for saithe in the sea lochs of the Firth of Clyde along with *Hercules II*. This fishery could produce single tows of up to 150 boxes of fish. On a good night, two tows would fill both boats with a combined catch of around 300 boxes. Like *Seeker*, *Wanderer* became still more versatile later in her career, spending part of her time creel fishing, for which purpose a McKay & McLeod creel hauler was fitted in 1978.

The evolution of the 40ft boats reached something of a peak in 1971 with the delivery of *Spes Bona II* (BA107). She was like a half-sized version of the big seiner/trawlers being built in north-east Scotland, though her cabin was forward instead of in the aft position normal on the new seiner/trawlers. This was to maximise the boat's capacity for carrying herring. When *Spes Bona II* was built, her owners contemplated the possibility of going to the ring net with her though this was an option that was never taken up.

Spes Bona II was fitted out for both the seine net and trawl and had a power block mounted on the aft side of her wheelhouse. Unlike all but one of her predecessors, she had a transom stern, giving her extra space aft. Most remarkably, her Caterpillar engine delivered no less than 200hp, which was an exceptional amount of power for a 40ft boat at the beginning of the seventies. *Spes Bona II*'s owners had seen the 200hp Caterpillar installed aboard Nobles' 54ft (16.46m) *Jasmine* (BA55) when she was re-engined in 1968 and realised that the engine could be accommodated aboard a 40-footer. *Spes Bona II*'s fishing activities included an outstanding haul at the cod fishing in the Clyde, taken in a tow of only fourteen minutes' duration. *Spes Bona II* had shot on a good mark and was towing on it when another mark appeared on her echo sounder. She kept on towing and was rewarded with a catch which totalled ninety-eight boxes of gutted cod and sixteen boxes of roe.

Mention must also be made of *Radiance* (BA289), delivered by Nobles to Girvan Skipper J. Johnston in 1966. This was one of the first transom-sterned, forward wheelhouse boats to join the Scottish inshore fleet. The majority of Nobles' fishing vessels had been aft wheelhouse, cruiser-sterned or canoe-sterned boats but the construction of *Radiance* demonstrated the yard's willingness and ability to build fishing vessels to completely new designs. The then unusual design was employed partly at the instigation of the White Fish Authority, which was actively promoting the construction of vessels of this type to modernise the white fish fleet. Skipper Johnston initially had his reservations about this, being one of many skippers who felt that a transom-sterned boat does not handle as well as a cruiser-sterned vessel when running before a following sea. He was persuaded to try the transom stern by colleagues who said that it was what lay below the waterline that counted and not what lay above it, though at Skipper Johnston's request, *Radiance*'s transom was not completely flat but shaped to an arc. Peter Noble suspects his father was among those who influenced Skipper Johnston as the transom stern featuring an arc was a characteristic of yachts built by James A. Silver at Rosneath.

In practice it was found that the forward wheelhouse had the drawback of making the helmsman suffer the maximum possible motion of the boat in a choppy sea. Despite this, *Radiance* proved to be an exceptionally good sea boat with a remarkable ability to cope with bad weather. When owned by Skipper Johnston, she spent much of her time dredging for clams out of West Loch Tarbert. This meant that every Monday she left Girvan and headed round the Mull of Kintyre to get to the fishing grounds. At the end of the week she came back around the Mull to get home.

On only two occasions over a two-year period did *Radiance* encounter weather sufficiently bad to stop her making her usual Monday passage and only once was she forced by bad weather to abandon the run home. She certainly had a good grip of the water: her draft was no less then 7½ft (2.3m).

However successful the 40-footers may have been, Nobles will always be best known for the construction of larger vessels intended primarily for ring net fishing. Nobles' first vessel of this type was the 54ft *Integrity* (BA335), built for T. & W. Shields Girvan in 1948. Nobles delivered a 55-footer, *Elizabeth Campbell* (CN186) in January 1950 but the termination of the post-Second World War Grant & Loan Scheme in 1950 led to the end of a boom in the construction of ring netters.

Despite this setback, Nobles won another order which led to the delivery in 1951 of the privately-financed *Saffron* (BA182) to J. & T. McCrindle of Maidens. With an overall length of 57½ft (17.6m) this highly successful ringer was a couple of feet longer than the biggest of the ring net boats which had been delivered up to that time. *Saffron*'s 152hp Gardner engine also made her a very powerful vessel for her time and gave her an impressive speed of 10 knots. A large number of 152hp Gardner engines were installed in fishing vessels throughout the fifties but these installations were almost always in boats between 65ft and 80ft long and not in 57-footers. *Saffron* was beamier than earlier ringers and her increased length and breadth allowed extra space in her forward cabin accommodation and raised her carrying capacity to 200 crans.

Saffron's design formed the basis of the larger and still more powerful ring net vessels which Nobles began to build in the 1960s. As early as 1957, Nobles produced a larger version of the *Saffron* hull. This was the 59ft (18m) *Summer Morn* (B78), which was built with a ring netter-type layout and had a varnished hull like the ringers. This vessel was, however, a seiner that never fished with the ring net. The reason for the forward cabin was the preference of her owners. When the ringers began to get bigger in the sixties, the largest of these boats were usually 58ft and 59ft overall and one vessel, the *Crystal Sea* (OB104), had an overall length of 60ft. As early as January 1962, Nobles launched their first 200hp ringer, the *Sapphire* (BA174), delivered to Angus and William McCrindle of Maidens. *Sapphire* was fitted with a Gardner 8L3B engine, the larger successor to the 152hp 8L3 model. Most of the ringers built by Nobles in the sixties had engines which developed between 150 and 200hp.

One of the other ringers built in the sixties deserves special mention. The 59ft, 200hp, *True Token* (B600) was one of the often-forgotten fleet of Northern Irish ringers based in Portavogie. Skippered by David Adair, her ring net partner was *Glorious* (B428) built by Palmers at Portavogie. Nobles had another representative among the Irish ringers as the older *Elizabeth Campbell*, when registered as B58, also ring netted from Portavogie in partnership with the Weatherhead-built *Trade Winds* (B27).

At the beginning of the seventies, Nobles' ringers became still larger and more powerful. *Westerlea* (OB93) and *Ribhinn Donn II* (SY141) were 63ft (19m) long. The ring net boats began to regularly install 230hp Gardner and 240hp Kelvin engines. Right at the end of ringer construction, the engine power of these vessels became greater still. At 55ft (17m) long, *Prospector* (BA25) was not especially large, but she had a 300hp Caterpillar engine. The 60ft (18m) *Alliance* (CN187) had a 365hp Caterpillar engine.

Ribhinn Donn II (SY141) had an unusual layout. Ring net vessels normally have their accommodation forward; fish hold amidships and engine room aft. The midships position of the hold made the ringers good carriers but the forward accommodation had its drawbacks in bad weather. The motion of the boat in particularly rough weather, for example when crossing the Minch in winter, could be so extreme as to force the crew out of the fo'c'sle to the aft wheelhouse or even the engine room. *Ribhinn Donn II* was designed to avoid this problem by having her cabin aft and her 230hp Gardner engine forward. To counter the weight of the engine forward, two fuel tanks were situated as far aft as possible. The layout made the accommodation much more comfortable for the crew and easier to access from the wheelhouse, though the trip for'ard to check on the engine could be fraught with hazard in bad weather.

Peter Noble considers that *Ribhinn Donn II* was the ultimate development of ring netter design though, somewhat ironically, this vessel never actually fished with a ring net and spent all her time trawling.

Throughout the second half of the fifties and the 1960s, the ring net boats became increasingly multi-purpose, being equipped not only for ring netting but also for prawn trawling or seine netting. The vessels engaged in prawning or seining from about the end of March to early summer in between herring seasons. Latterly, herring pair trawling became another option. This allowed the boats to work in more open waters than their close-inshore ring net haunts and was one of the main reasons for their steadily increasing engine power. The newer vessels had increased carrying capacity as well as versatility – the 63-footers could carry 280 crans of herring.

Some skippers to whom the authors have spoken consider that these benefits brought with them certain disadvantages and that boats above 60ft in length were not ideal for ring net operations. The drawback of the larger boats was their tendency to catch the wind more than smaller vessels. This in turn could push the boat away from the net, heaving the bottom of it up through a shoal of herring before the net could be properly closed and the fish trapped. This problem might have been capable of being resolved. Peter Noble thought the only way of advancing ringer design beyond *Ribhinn Donn II* would have been to fit side thrusters. This was never attempted but his logic was that if it was possible to pierce the hull of a wooden boat to fit sonar, there was no reason why tunnels for side thrusters could not have been fitted as well. Thrusters are a great aid to manoeuvrability and one of the endemically manoeuvrable ring net boats with side thrusting propellers would have been an exceptionally nimble vessel and better able to resist the effects of the wind when she was fishing.

The ringers' wheelhouses also became larger to accommodate the increasing amount of electronic, radio and other equipment which was fitted to the newer fishing vessels. *Westerlea* was one of the most comprehensively equipped boats. She had a Norwinch hydraulic trawl winch, a Hydema hydraulic ring net winch and an AKA power block. Her wheelhouse electrics included an Elac Mittel Lodar sonar, a Simrad 160 echo sounder, a Woodson Clipper 50 radio telephone, a Decca Navigator, a Decca 250 autopilot and a Kelvin Hughes Type 17 radar. *Westerlea* had accommodation for an unusually large crew of nine with seven bunks in the main cabin forward and another two bunks in a compartment aft of the engine room.

Prospector is renowned as the only transom-sterned ringer ever built. In practice she only fished with the ring net for two winters in the Minch, though in the 1973/74 season she was credited with being one of the best-fished boats in the fleet. Her partner was Nobles' *Stormdrift* (BA187) and the two boats spent much of their time at the ring net in a four-boat team with two more of Nobles' ringers, *Sapphire* and *Silver Quest* (BA302). *Stormdrift* and *Silver Quest* seem at times to have been the lucky boats in this team – on one occasion they returned to the east coast of South Uist after landing in Mallaig and it took them no more than five minutes to find the herring again. Their shot, taken at the mouth of Loch Skiport, totalled 300 crans.

Prospector showed that a transom-sterned vessel could be used successfully for ring netting, though the transom stern did have a drawback. *Prospector* was a competent but not exceptional carrier with a capacity for 170 crans of herring. A large engine room required for her big engine and a spacious cabin forward cut down her hold space and the buoyancy of the transom stern was such that *Prospector's* stern tended to ride high in the water, even when she was loaded. This tended to push her head down and it would have been preferable if her stern had gone down a little more to bring her head up for better sea-keeping when crossing the Minch.

The transom stern also proved to have an advantage. When the boats were fishing very close inshore it was common for *Stormdrift* to shoot her net. During hauling, *Prospector's* stern was lashed to *Stormdrift's* side and *Prospector* used her big engine power to keep her partner off the nearby rocks. The transom stern made it much easier for *Prospector* to manoeuvre her partner, holding fast against *Stormdrift* when a cruiser stern would have tended to slide along *Stormdrift's* side. Skipper Willie Anderson of *Prospector* credits his boat's capabilities in this regard with having saved several big hauls of herring that could not otherwise have been taken when the fish were extremely close to the shore.

With the ring net era drawing towards a close, it was fitting that Nobles' yard, which had made a speciality out of building ringers, built the last boat to be constructed to a ringer design. This was the Campbeltown-based *Alliance* (CN187), though she spent only one week fishing unsuccessfully with the ring net in Kilbrannan Sound in partnership with *Silver Cloud* (CN267) (built by Fairlie Yacht Slip) and spent most of her fishing career trawling.

A study of the history of Nobles' ringers demonstrates that they had a penchant for innovation beyond their generally increasing size, power and versatility already remarked upon. *Crystal Sea* and *Pathfinder* (BA252), built in 1963 and 1964 respectively, were early examples of inshore fishing vessels with hydraulic trawl winches, a Fordsmith Brixham unit aboard *Crystal Sea* and Norwinch aboard *Pathfinder*.

In the summer of 1968, *Crystal Sea* was one of the first vessels in the Scottish inshore fleet to be fitted with a hydraulic power block which was mounted on a crane fitted to the aft side of her wheelhouse. *Crystal Sea* used her power block to experiment with the mechanised hauling of ring nets and also experimented with a small purse seine.

Pathfinder was another vessel to experiment with power block hauling of ring nets though she did so in a completely different way from *Crystal Sea*. In the early seventies, *Pathfinder* was fitted with two pedestal-mounted power blocks on her port side, one forward and one aft. These were used to haul a 145 fathom by 50 fathom ring net. While some effort was devoted to developing satisfactory methods of mechanised hauling for ring nets, these met with no great measure of success. *Crystal Sea* proved that she could fish with a small purse seine and a later purse seining experiment by *Westerlea* demonstrated that she could effectively wield a larger 220 fathom by 60 fathom purse net, but vessels of their size fished more readily with a ring net or herring pair trawl than a purse seine. *Pathfinder* and her regular partner, Nobles' *Ocean Gem* (BA265), fished so successfully at the ring net and pair trawl as to finance their replacement by an 89ft, Norwegian-built purse seiner, *Pathfinder* (BA188) in 1973. *Crystal Sea* and one of her partners, Nobles' *Silvery Sea* (OB156), were also replaced by a purse seiner in 1973. This was the 87ft, Dutch-built *Crystal Sea II* (OB145). In 1979 *Westerlea's* owners, Peter McLean & partners made the switch to purse seining when they bought the Dutch-built *Azalea* (LK193) second hand.

One of the more successful attempts to partially mechanise the hauling of a ring net did not involve the use of a power block. *Silver Quest* fished with a net which had a spring rope attached to its cork line in addition to the spring rope on the foot of the net. Ten plastic rings were attached to the cork line with beckets linking these to the spring rope. The cork line spring rope was hauled around the drums on *Silver Quest's* seine net winch while the spring rope on the foot of the net was hauled using the ring net winch in the normal fashion. This procedure allowed *Silver Quest* to haul her net in weather conditions that would otherwise have been impossible to work in. Skipper Bob McCutcheon of *Silver Quest* remembers getting several good hauls which he credits to the spring rope on the cork line, including one of 600 baskets of herring taken on Lady Isle Bank in the Firth of Clyde when working in partnership with *Sapphire*.

Ring net skippers from the island of Eriskay, who for a time operated two of Nobles' boats, also came up with an alteration to the design of ring nets which is well worth recording. This was a ring net specially adapted for catching mackerel by the removal of the wide mesh from the foot of the net to avoid heavy meshings of fish which were commonly a problem when ringing for mackerel. Meshings of mackerel in ordinary ring nets could be so heavy that the net became virtually impossible to handle and one skipper who tried to catch mackerel with an un-adapted ring net described the results as 'a disaster'. The altered ring net avoided this difficulty and fished well, though the team had only one such net and accordingly the same boat was shooting all the time.

In 1971 the team was joined by Nobles' *Jasper* (SY379) which was re-named *Santa Maria III* (CY38) and, in 1973, another Noble-built boat, *Silvery Sea*, was acquired by the Mackinnons of Eriskay. *Silvery Sea* became *Regina Maris* (CY105) and she and *Santa Maria III*, along with their partners, the Weatherhead & Blackie-built *Ave Maria* (CY1) and *Santa Maria II* (CY290) are probably the best remembered of the Eriskay boats.

The Eriskay ringers fished for mackerel during the months of August, September and October, from around 1970 to 1975. The fish were close inshore from Sandray northwards to the Barra Sound on ideal fishing grounds for the ringers. The fishery was remarkably consistent in producing very large rings of 600/700 crans. These were often taken just before daylight and it was common for one ring to catch so much fish as to either fill all four boats or at least give all four a worthwhile cargo to take to the market at Mallaig. In the early years of the fishery, the Eriskay ringers virtually had the fishing to themselves. In later years herring became increasingly scarce in the Minch, especially at the start of the winter season, and much of the Scottish herring fleet made up for poor herring fishing by catching mackerel in the early part of the season. With pressure of fishing by big pair trawlers and purse seiners mounting, the mackerel shoals became increasingly fragmented and fast moving and the ringers were edged out of the fishery.

It is conspicuous that Nobles' ringers were well represented among the last boats to fish with the ring net as the ring net fishing came to its end in the second half of the seventies. In the early seventies, ring net boats became increasingly inclined to pair trawl for herring as pressure of fishing scattered the shoals and led to the fish becoming faster moving and harder to catch with ring nets. Growing numbers of Clyde ringers turned to the pair trawl when herring fishing on their home grounds. In the Minch, some boats carried both ring nets and pair trawls at the same time so they could fish by either method as fishing conditions required. By the mid-seventies, many of these boats were carrying trawls only. This applied even in ring net strongholds such as Scalpay. Nobles' *Village Maid* (SY63) and *Vigilant* (SY28), both built for Scalpay owners, were trawling by the winter of 1973/74, though they did not pair together and instead worked with east-coast-built partners. *Village Maid* teamed up with *Britannia* (SY6) while *Vigilant* teamed up with *Scalpay Isle III* (SY19) and *Jasper* (SY460).

By 1975, there was an inconsequential amount of ring net activity in the Clyde. The only remaining ring net fishery of any substance was the winter fishing in the Minch and this fishery was a shadow of its former self.

Ocean Gem was last in the Minch as late as the winter of 1974/75, pairing with the Sandhaven-built *Britannia* (BA267). *Aliped VIII* (BA155) and *Aliped IX* (BA234) (the *Alipeds*) were active with the ring net until the winter of 1975/76. *Stormdrift, Marie* (BA211) and *Silver Quest* were ringing in the Minch as late as the winter of 1976/77, working in a four-boat team with the Macduff-built *Chrysolyte* (BA301). This was the last team of Clyde ringers to go to the ring net fishing in the Minch. Their last big haul in the Minch was a huge ring of herring taken in *Chrysolyte*'s net off the mouth of

Loch Uskavagh and which filled all four boats. *Chrysolyte* took 180 crans aboard from this catch, *Silver Quest* carried 160 crans, *Marie* took 200 crans and *Stormdrift* loaded up with 220 crans. With all four of the ringers full, there were still fish left in the net and these had to be released. There is no way of knowing how much herring remained in the net but it is hard to see how this catch could have been less than 800 crans.

The last catch of all taken by the foursome in the Minch was another shot with *Chrysolyte*'s net between the islands of Floddaybeg, Floddaymore and Haunaray off North Uist. *Stormdrift* missed what might have been a big haul that day as she found a good mark of herring when steaming down the shore in the wrong direction to allow her to shoot her net. The shoal disappeared very quickly and the team could not re-locate it but *Chrysolyte* shot on a different mark and took a respectable catch of 70 crans.

Regina Maris and *Santa Maria III* persevered at the ring net until the 1977/78 winter season, still fishing in a four-boat team with *Ave Maria* and *Santa Maria II* and this was probably the last team to fish commercially with the ring net. They continued to make some use of ring nets after the Minch herring fishing was closed for a three-year period from July 1978, but they were not fishing commercially. For a fortnight each year until the fishing re-opened in 1981, fisheries scientists chartered the Eriskay ringers to catch herring for tagging and other scientific purposes.

While the Eriskay ringers are widely thought to be the last boats to use ring nets for commercial fishing, the identity of the last commercial ringer is not beyond doubt. There was another ring net team fishing in the winter of 1977/78 and Nobles had built both boats. *Pathfinder* was by then re-registered as OB181 and had been partnering *Westerlea* for some years though the team had come to concentrate on pair trawling when catching herring. In that last winter of ring net fishing in the Minch, the presence of herring marks close inshore led to *Westerlea*'s ring net being taken back aboard. She carried both the ring net and a trawl while *Pathfinder* was carrying trawls only.

In practice little use was made of the ring net though *Westerlea* did shoot it. She had one relatively unsuccessful shot in Billy's Bight at the mouth of Loch Eynort. On another occasion she shot in breezy weather and with the big ringer catching the wind, *Pathfinder* had to push her partner to windward to make it physically possible for *Westerlea*'s crew to haul the ring net. The team's search for herring later took them into Broadford Bay, Skye, and this led to an incident which more than amply demonstrates the unpredictability of herring shoals.

On arriving in Broadford Bay in daylight, the boats found marks of fish on the bottom that were thought to be sprats. One of *Pathfinder*'s pair trawls was fitted with a sprat bag and the team tried a tow with this net. They caught no sprats but instead took several boxes of the biggest herring Skipper Peter MacLean of *Westerlea* had ever seen and, most remarkably, the fish were all this size. The bay was full of herring marks and the skippers reasoned that if these formed up and rose from the bottom with the coming of darkness, then a very big fishing was in prospect. *Westerlea* and *Pathfinder* lay in Broadford until the approach of nightfall and then went in search of the shoals which had earlier been detected. Astonishingly, these could not be found again. Despite the volume of fish that had earlier been present, the bay was now barren and an extensive search of the whole area by the sonar-equipped east-coast pair trawlers *Mystic* (FR124), *Wistaria* (FR116), *Adventurer* (INS8) and *Vision* (PD138) also failed to locate the fish. How such substantial quantities of herring contrived to disappear completely remains a mystery. It is also rather a pity since, if *Westerlea* had taken a last big ring from the marks which had been seen, her ring net swansong might have produced an extremely large catch.

One of the last ring net pairs, photographed with their herring pair trawls aboard. On the left is the Macduff-built *Chrysolyte* (BA301) and on the right Nobles' *Silver Quest* (BA302). (The late Mrs M. J.M. Drummond)

Alliance and *Aquila* in Tarbert with their big haul of sprats. (Courtesy Lenny McLaughlin)

Possibly the most unexpected instance of late ring net activity took place in the winter of 1975/76 when *Sapphire* took part in the Cornish mackerel fishery with a ring net. She was at that time owned by Barry West of Falmouth in Cornwall, though she retained her Ballantrae registration. *Sapphire* was partnered by the St Monance-built *Village Belle III* (CN44), which went south from the Clyde to join up with *Sapphire* for the winter season. The boats began fishing in late September, but the mackerel were scattered and fast moving. This led to very light catches with some shots producing next to nothing. It was hoped that when the mackerel marks became thicker and slower moving the ring net boats would fish well. However, results over the winter were generally disappointing and the experiment was not repeated. Both ringers returned to Scotland, *Sapphire* being sold to Skipper John Galbraith of Carradale in July 1976.

A number of Nobles' ringers continued fishing for herring with pair trawls after the demise of the ring net. Examples include the *Alipeds*, *Village Belle IV*, *Village Maid II*, *Westerlea*, *Pathfinder*, *Sapphire*, *Stormdrift*, *Marie*, *Prospector* and *Silver Quest*. When the Minch herring fishing closed, many of Nobles' Clyde-based ex-ringers remained loyal to the herring fishing and continued pair trawling for herring, in some cases right up to the demise of the Clyde herring fishing itself. *Santa Maria III* and *Regina*

Maris returned to the herring fishing in the Minch when the fishery re-opened in July 1981, though they were by then fishing with mid-water trawls and not ring nets. Had the herring been close inshore in shallow water the boats might have gone back to the ringing but the grounds tight to the shore where the ringers had at times fished so well proved to be barren after the three-year closure. *Santa Maria III* and *Regina Maris* made their catches in deeper water on the Coll and Curachan Banks. They managed to catch some good quality herring but tight quotas severely restricted their activities at this fishery.

As the ringers spent increasingly more time pair trawling, vessels with 200hp and more proved to have a decided advantage over less powerful boats, though the re-engining of some of the older boats, such as the installation of 310hp Kelvin engines in the *Alipeds* in 1974 and 335hp Caterpillar engines in *Stormdrift* and *Marie* in 1978, gave these boats a catching power on a par with newer vessels. Some of these vessels also pair trawled for sprats while others used their mid-water pair trawls to catch saithe in the Firth of Clyde. These fisheries could produce some very big catches for the size of vessels involved. During the best of the saithe fishing, both the *Aliped* team and *Chrysolyte* and *Silver Quest* took hauls of over 300 boxes. The sprat fishing produced the best trawl catch by a Nobles' pair known to the authors. This was a massive 70-tonne shot landed at Tarbert by *Aquila* (OB99) and *Alliance* in December 1982. The catch was taken in three tows, the biggest of which was a 36-tonne haul in *Aquila*'s net.

Impressive as the big sprat catch may be, it was still considerably smaller than some of the huge single rings which the ring net boats could take in the big years of the herring fishing. The problem about recording big single rings is that these were invariably much bigger than one boat or even a pair could carry and had to be divided among several boats. There are usually no written records of these catches and memories of them are fading. *Jasmine* took a huge ring off Peter's Port, Loch Uskavagh that Skipper Willie Anderson remembers as filling six or seven boats. If we take a conservative line and assume it was six boats with capacity for 150 crans each, then the big ring cannot have been less than 900 crans. It may have exceeded 1,000 crans. *Jasmine* did so well at the ring net that she was filled to the hatches with around 160/170 crans of herring sixty-five times when fishing in the Minch. This is known for certain because one of her crew kept a diary record of occasions when she was filled to capacity. *Crystal Sea*'s team, consisting of herself, *Silvery Sea* and the Weatherhead-built *Mary Manson* (OB70), *Margaret Ann* (OB79) and *Maggie McLean* (OB174), were occasionally all filled with one ring. As the boats in the team could carry between 180 crans and 230 crans, a ring which filled them all, had to be in the vicinity of 1,000 crans.

One of the most clearly remembered big rings is also the most unexpected. When little *Dalriada* went to the Kessock herring fishery in 1966, she damaged her net on her first night's fishing. The crew mended the tear in the net and *Dalriada* put straight back to sea. This time she took a colossal ring that was far more than she could handle, even assisted by her partners *Caledonia* and *Nancy Glen*. The combined crews of the three boats quite simply could not get hold of the bag, which was almost solid with herring. The three 40-footers needed help from two east-coast boats, the drifter *Accumulator* (INS215) and the ringer *Maggie McLeman II* (INS270), which were also strapped to the bag. The five boats took 500 crans out of the net and the rest of the catch was set free. Skipper Robert Ross of *Dalriada* is positive that the boats released at least as much fish as they had taken aboard. Accordingly, it is very probable that this ring was somewhere in excess of 1,000 crans, a remarkable achievement for a 40-footer. *Nancy Glen's* skipper compared the catch to the hauls taken by the Norwegian purse seiners in the North Sea and with some justification – a Norwegian purser would have been very happy with a 1,000-cran ring.

The authors are delighted to conclude this brief account of monster ring net hauls with a ring by a Nobles' boat which definitely exceeded 1,000 crans. This was taken in The Carreag, west of Bay Harty in the Calvay Sound on the east coast of South Uist. The vessel responsible was Eriskay skipper Calum Mackinnon's *Santa Maria III*. Slightly differing versions of this story maintain that six or seven ringers were filled from this one ring and the authors think they have identified six of them. The catch was shared among *Santa Maria III*; the three other Eriskay-based and Weatherhead-built ringers *Ave Maria*, *Santa Maria II* and *Santa Maria* (CY144); two other Nobles' ringers, the Tarbert-based *Village Belle IV* and *Village Maid II* and possibly a seventh boat which has remained unidentified. Let us be conservative and assume there were six boats. All accounts agree that the boats were filled from the net. This is supported by one eyewitness who remembers the Eriskay crews encouraging the Tarbert men to take more fish out of the net. The reply was along the lines of: 'We're full. Where do we put more? In the bunks?' Let us also assume that 'filled' means 200 crans aboard five modern ringers and a more modest 150 crans aboard the older *Santa Maria* which was built in 1948. Simple arithmetic tells us that the catch could not be less than 1,000 crans and had to be appreciably more. Interestingly, this massive ring was taken very late in the ring net era. It was in the early 1970s, during the last years of the big herring fishing in the Minch.

In light of the various stories about big rings related to the authors and on a scrutiny of these, it seems quite possible that more than one of Nobles' ringers took single shots of 1,000 crans of herring. Maybe, just maybe, *Santa Maria III* took the biggest catch ever by a ring net boat. At the very least it seems possible that she took the biggest single ring where all of the catch was saved and no fish were lost due to the net bursting or to part of the catch having to be deliberately released.

Perhaps the last word on Nobles' ringers is best left for Skipper Grieve Gemmell of *Stormdrift*. His assessment of his boat is: 'There was never a boat like her at sea so far as I'm concerned. They [Nobles] built marvellous boats. I would go anywhere in them.' If this is the ringers' valediction, they could scarcely have a better one.

While Nobles had concentrated largely on building ring netters and varying types of 40-footers, the yard also built fishing boats of other types, including several small trawlers for owners in the Isle of Man. Some of these were variations on the ring netter design. Others, such as *Fenella Ann* (CT27) and *Rebena Belle* (CT63), were forward wheelhouse stern trawlers. *Fenella Ann* was unusual in having two propulsion engines.

Rebena Belle loaded with herring. (Courtesy Lenny McLaughlin)

She had an 88hp Kelvin main engine and a 66hp Kelvin wing engine which could work in tandem. This type of layout was commonly found in inshore boats in Cornwall but was rare in the more northerly parts of Britain. When *Rebena Belle* had been sold into Irish ownership and re-registered as N313, she indulged in a remarkable piece of herring catching at the Mourne drift net fishery. On this occasion she returned to Kilkeel full of herring with even her deck covered in fish. The little boat landed no less than 110 crans for her night's work.

One complete departure from any other Nobles design was the 70ft (21m) drifter *Faithful* (PD307) that was built for Skipper George Forman & Partners of Peterhead in 1953. Nobles won the order for *Faithful* as a result of a visit to north-east Scotland by Alexander Noble at a time when a new grant and loan scheme had been introduced to encourage the building of new fishing vessels and a considerable number of orders were being placed with various east-coast yards for the construction of seiner/drifters. *Faithful* was much larger than any vessel previously built by Nobles and her size caused a disconcerting problem when she grounded in Girvan Harbour straight after her launch by Miss Jane Forman, the sister of Skipper George Forman. It had originally been intended to launch *Faithful* rather cautiously due to her size, though Skipper Forman recollects the boat sliding into the water with some panache notwithstanding the plan for her launch. This did not cause any problem, but when *Faithful* was manoeuvring in the harbour under her own power she ran aground even at high water. Happily, *Faithful* was able to free herself using her seine net winch which coped with the unexpected strain despite concerns that this might damage the brand new equipment.

Faithful was named after a steam drifter owned by Skipper Forman's grandfather, albeit after a ballot among her owners to choose the name. She was a fine sea boat and did well at the drift net but even better things were to come when she became one of the first Scottish vessels to successfully pair trawl for herring. In 1964, *Faithful's* owners built the larger *Venture* (PD72) at the Peterhead boatyard of Richard Irvin & Sons Ltd, while retaining ownership of *Faithful*. *Venture* was powered by a 240hp Kelvin engine and *Faithful* had been re-engined in 1958 with an 180hp Kelvin, so the two boats had adequate power to pair trawl in 1964. Command of *Faithful* passed briefly to Skipper Forman's father, John, and following his retirement from the sea for health reasons, to Skipper Walter Milne.

Faithful and *Venture* first used the herring pair trawl in the autumn of 1964 at the East Anglian fishing and in the winter of 1965/66 they were among the first pair trawlers to work in the Minch. Their initial attempts at pair trawling were generally unsuccessful due in substantial part to what was thought to be a wrongly rigged net, though they took a 140 cran herring catch off Lochmaddy. When the partners first went to the pair trawl they had neither trawl winches nor gallows and hauled their nets with their seine net winches using ropes instead of wire warps. This led to a frightening incident on board *Faithful* when a rope jumped out of a roller and swept two of her crew over the side. Fortunately, both men were rescued, but after that, the boats were more thoroughly adapted for trawling with new winches and trawl gallows. They also had larger engines installed: a 320hp Kelvin in *Venture* and a 240hp Kelvin in *Faithful*, though *Faithful* would have had a 320hp engine had Herring Industry Board grant assistance been forthcoming. *Venture* was always the more powerful of the two and always towed the 'heavy end', taking the starboard side of the trawl which meant that with her starboard side gallows, the wires reached into the sea right across her stern, instead of running into the water more or less directly aft from the gallows.

Faithful and *Venture* began to do well at the pair trawl. *Venture* had a single haul of 320 crans of herring in her net and *Faithful* later had one of 400 crans. The two partners also fished for a time in a multi-boat team. Peterhead's Big Five herring team was one of the most successful of all the herring pair trawlers. The team consisted of several different boats at different times but possibly the classic Big Five comprised the east-coast-built *Shemara* (PD325), *Fairweather IV* (PD107), *Juneve* (PD432), *Sparkling Star* (PD108) and *Ugievale II* (PD105). It is, however, commonly forgotten that the first Big Five consisted of *Shemara*, *Fairweather* (PD197), *Juneve*, *Venture* and Nobles' *Faithful*.

Walter Milne replaced *Faithful* with the Fairmile-built *Faithful II* (PD67) in 1971. *Faithful* was re-named *Be Faithful* (B10) and continued to spend a substantial part of her time successfully pair trawling for herring, with the Buckie-built *Fragrant Rose*

(B74). When *Faithful II* and *Be Faithful* were fishing in the Clyde with their respective partners, it was occasionally possible to find the old *Faithful* and her replacement lying companionably together in Ayr Harbour while the two skippers swapped information about the fishing.

As ring net fishing declined in the 1970s, demand for ring net craft lessened and ultimately ceased. Responding to the changing demands of the fishing vessel market, Nobles began to build more different types of vessel, many of which were similar to the seiner/trawlers built on the Scottish east coast.

Spindrift (BA220), delivered to Skipper Donald McLean of Maidens in 1974, was the first of the new generation of boats, though she was in some respects a hybrid vessel and in this boat's design one can see the ring netter evolving into a seiner/trawler. This was partly by design and partly something that happened when *Spindrift* was being built. Her hull was designed to be essentially the same as *Prospector*. Both vessels were intended to be just below 25 tons measured under Part IV of the Merchant Shipping Act 1894. This was to allow the boats to be taken to sea by a skipper who did not hold a Skipper's Certificate or a Second Hand (Special) Certificate under the Merchant Shipping Acts 1894 to 1965. While *Spindrift* was under construction, Donald McLean obtained a Skipper's Certificate. Nobles felt the vessel would benefit from an extra plank to give greater freeboard and, with the 25 gross tonnage limit no longer being a problem, a decision was taken to amend the design. This led to some of the shorter frames being extended in order to accommodate the extra planking.

Spindrift's wheelhouse was a development of what had become something of a Nobles' classic. Several of the last of Nobles' ring net boats had wheelhouses of composite construction. The after part of their deckhouses were of steel while the wheelhouses themselves were of wood sheathed on the outside with teak, which gave a most attractive and distinctive appearance. *Spindrift*'s wheelhouse was of this type, but was a larger version, with the galley in the deckhouse aft of the wheelhouse. Her crew accommodation was aft and she had a whaleback forward. Aft accommodation was rare on a ring net boat and whalebacks were unknown on ringers but both of these features had become standard on seiner/trawlers. When new, *Spindrift* was fully rigged as a seiner/trawler. She spent an appreciable amount of time pair trawling for herring both in the Clyde and at the Isle of Man with the Buckie-built *Laurisa* (BA145), though she spent most of her fishing career bottom trawling for prawns or white fish.

Nobles' next delivery, *Wanderer II* (BA76), confirmed the yard's ability to build east-coast-style seiner/trawlers. *Wanderer II* was a hefty 69-footer, built for David and Kenny Gibson of Dunure who had done so well with their 40ft *Wanderer* that they were able to replace her with a much larger vessel. At first, some doubts were expressed about the viability of the big boat on the Clyde grounds and her owners initially found some difficulty in recruiting experienced seine net crewmen for her. In practice, *Wanderer II* proved so effective at the seine net that she became one of the most successful fishing vessels based in the Firth of Clyde. After three years her owners had a waiting list of men wanting to join her crew. She was built with seine net rope storage bins so her crew were spared the tedious task of carrying coils of seine net rope around the deck. *Wanderer II* became even more pleasant to operate when she was fitted with rope storage reels, which proved superior to the bins in all respects. The reels avoided the heavy wear on the ropes caused by the bins and a seiner with rope reels can work with none of the crew on the foredeck at all during much of the fishing operation.

In a way, *Wanderer II* was badly named because, as long as she carried that name, she didn't wander at all, having virtually no need to stray from her home grounds where she almost always worked a four-day week. She devoted nearly all of her time to the seine net but was fitted out for both seine netting and trawling and did spend a few weeks bottom trawling during the big years of the seasonal cod fishing in the Clyde. Her exploits at the seine net included an enormous single shot of 390 boxes of dogfish and 150 boxes of other species taken south-west of Ailsa Craig on a Thursday morning. Her activities at the cod included an outstanding £22,000 grossing for one of her four-day weeks. At the time, this would have been a very big grossing for one of the big east-coast seiner/trawlers fishing in the North Sea. These boats were much larger than *Wanderer II*, between 80 and 85ft in length and would probably be at sea for around double the length of *Wanderer's* trip to achieve such a grossing.

The yard built four more vessels of the same general type as *Wanderer II*. Three of these, *Alison Mary* (N308), *Rose of Sharon M* (N349), and *Rambling Rose* (N359) were trawlers for Irish owners. All three had beautifully varnished hulls. These had been typical of the ringers and 40-footers which Nobles had once built, but unusual on larger vessels, especially trawlers, whose hulls were more prone to wear and tear than that sustained by ringers and seiners. *Alison Mary* had an enlarged version of the composite wood/steel wheelhouse but she was the last boat to include this feature. All of Nobles' other fishing boats from *Wanderer II* onwards had all-metal wheelhouses in east-coast style.

Devorgilla (BA67) was the most versatile of the bigger class of seiner/trawlers, being capable of seining, trawling and scallop dredging. When new, she spent most of her time engaged in different forms of trawling. She went demersal trawling for prawns; single-boat pelagic trawling for hake and other white fish in the North Channel; herring pair trawling in the Clyde with the Macduff-built *Silver Harvest* (BA130) and single-boat pelagic trawling for mackerel off Cornwall. *Devorgilla's* one season at the Cornish mackerel was in the winter of 1978/79 and was classed by her skipper, David Smith, as a failure due to lengthy spells of bad weather which forced the boat to seek shelter in Penzance Harbour and a lorry drivers' strike which hampered the disposal of her catches. Nevertheless, *Devorgilla* still managed to demonstrate what a Nobles' 70-footer could do at the mackerel when she took a colossal single haul of 120 tonnes from a tow which lasted between ten and twenty minutes. In later years as *Harvester* (PD98) she added another form of trawling to her activities, successfully pair trawling for white fish with the Bangor-built *Ocean Harvest* (PD198).

The construction of this type of vessel by Nobles came to a peak in 1988 with the delivery of the 70ft *Margarets* (LH232) to Skipper David Fairnie of Fisherrow. *Margarets* was built for white fish pair trawling and single boat trawling, and her three-barrelled winch gave her the ability to work the twin-rig trawl. She was also the largest fishing vessel built by the yard, which had to construct a new slipway to launch her.

Despite her capability for twin-rig trawling, *Margarets* has spent most of her career pair trawling, usually for white fish. She has had two different partners; both called *Nova Spero* (LH142) and built in Arbroath, one in 1973 and the other in 1987. On occasion the team has been forced to diversify their activities, either as a result of poor fishing or of taking its white fish quotas sufficiently quickly as to leave the boats short of fishing opportunities. This has led to *Margarets* spending a short amount of time at the prawns and also to a brief experiment pair trawling for sprats and herring. These fisheries had been traditional activities for the Fairnie family going back to the days of the ring net boats from the Firth of Forth. *Margarets'* brief spell at the herring has probably made her the last of Nobles' boats to fish for herring, once the primary activity of many vessels built by the yard. The absence of refrigerated seawater tanks prevented *Margarets* and *Nova Spero* from making a commercial success out of the herring. By the time they tried the fishery, the market was accustomed to fish caught by purse seiners and pelagic trawlers and carried in RSW and would not accept catches which had not had the benefit of transportation in seawater. Nevertheless, *Margarets* demonstrated her herring-catching capabilities more than adequately with a single shot of 700 boxes taken off Whitby and landed at Blyth.

Margarets' present skipper, Jamie Fairnie, is full of praise for his boat. Nobles are renowned for building extremely solid boats and *Margarets* is a prime example of this. Where her shelterdeck is bolted to her hull, she has three bolts where most boats have one. The hull itself is so solid that one surveyor who looked at *Margarets* asked if she had been strengthened for working in ice. Not a drop of leakage comes through her hull and her cabin stays totally dry. She took two years to build but is a superb example of the art of building fishing vessels in wood.

In its later years as a fishing-boat builder, the yard built a 38ft static netter *Moyallon* (OB24) for Skipper Nigel Johnston of Mallaig and a larger static net boat, the *L & T Britannia V* (FH121) for John Leach and Freddie Turner of Mevagissey in Cornwall. *L & T Britannia V* was rigged for gill netting and tangle netting and was equipped to stay at sea for four to six days, working up to 100 miles from port. She had a mizzen sail for keeping her head to the wind when working her gear totalling 600 nets. *L & T Britannia V* targeted turbot, monk, crawfish and hake with her tangle nets and pollack, ling and cod with her wreck nets.

L & T Britannia V fished successfully all round the British coast. *Moyallon's* capabilities as a fishing boat were marred by a series of legal cases regarding her tangle nets, which completely spoiled her career as a static netter.

The *Moyallon* case – or legal debacle, depending on one's viewpoint – centred around the issue of whether her tangle nets should properly be classed as gill nets for the purposes of the Inshore Fishing (Prohibition of Carriage of Monofilament Gill Nets) (Scotland) Order 1986 which had been made to inhibit the illegal catching of salmon. Skipper Nigel Johnston of *Moyallon* had received substantial Government assistance in the form of both Sea Fish Industry Authority grants and a Highlands and Islands Development Board loan towards the £140,000 cost of building *Moyallon* for gill net fishing. When the boat was only five months old, the new regulations were created and prohibited the carrying of gill nets within 6 miles of the Scottish coast. *Moyallon* was working off the north coast of Ireland, well outside the Scottish 6-mile limit, but the rules prohibited her from entering a Scottish port with her nets aboard even though vessels from other countries could dock in Scotland while carrying the exact same type of nets.

Skipper Johnston was first arrested for carrying illegal gill nets within 6 miles of the Scottish coast in 1987 but the charges against him were dropped. He was arrested again in March 1991 and charged with a contravention of Article 3 of the 1986 Order and of Sections 2 and 4 of the Inshore Fishing (Scotland) Act 1984 in respect that *Moyallon* had carried aboard a quantity of monofilament gill nets while in Mallaig Harbour. This was to lead to a two-year court battle, notwithstanding that the Crown conceded that the eleven-inch mesh nets were incapable of catching salmon and it was legal for English and Spanish fishing vessels to use such nets off the Scottish west coast.

Following the trial in January 1993, Sheriff Nolan found Skipper Johnston not guilty of the charges. This decision was overruled by the High Court on appeal by the Scottish Office. The case was remitted back to the Sheriff for sentencing. Sheriff Nolan admonished Skipper Johnston, saying that the skipper was heavily out of pocket as a result of the case and faced having to sell his boat. Skipper Johnston was indeed compelled to sell *Moyallon* and she is now fishing as a potter from Bridlington on the English east coast.

In 1985, Nobles made a major break from their tradition of building wooden vessels when they delivered the 38ft (11.5m), steel-hulled *Kingfisher II* (BA149) to Tony Medina of Ayr. James Noble and his son, Simon, had already built a small steel yacht in their spare time and experience of working in steel gained on this project was to prove invaluable in the construction of *Kingfisher*. Nobles originally thought of building *Kingfisher* in the open but instead opted to put up a new shed to accommodate her. While this shed no longer exists, it was later extended and used to build Nobles' first steel fishing boat.

Kingfisher, while registered as a fishing boat, was a sea angling craft. The first steel fishing boat built by Nobles was the 44ft stern trawler *Valaura* (BA256), launched for Skipper Donald McCrindle of Girvan in 1987. *Valaura* was built primarily for white fish and prawn trawling but her 260hp Gardner engine gave her sufficient power for the additional options of herring pair trawling and single-boat pelagic trawling for white fish. While one would expect a steel boat to have more internal space than a wooden vessel, *Valaura* was very spacious indeed, with 7ft of headroom for'ard, 10ft of headroom in her engine room, and a 360-box capacity fish hold.

Kingfisher. (Courtesy Alexander Noble & Sons Ltd, Girvan)

The building of *Valaura* conferred upon Nobles the distinction of being one of the few boatyards in Scotland to build fishing vessels in both wood and steel. A number of yards have delivered both wooden and steel fishing boats but these yards commonly subcontracted the construction of steel hulls and superstructures to other builders. Nobles achieved the rare feat of constructing both wooden and steel hulls themselves.

The diversification into building in steel went to some extent against the preferences of the Noble family, who had and still have a deeply ingrained tradition of craftsman-building high-quality vessels in wood. However, the move proved to be sound business sense as well as an effective demonstration of the yard's versatility. While Nobles could always find skippers wishing to build the yard's designs of traditional wooden vessels, increasing numbers of fishermen were building steel boats in the seventies and eighties.

Additionally, by the latter part of the eighties, fishing boat orders of any kind were becoming scarce throughout the entire United Kingdom. Nobles' last fishing boat for a considerable time was *Delta Dawn* (SY788), which began as a speculative building project and was delivered as a creeler/netter/trawler to Skipper Neil MacAulay from the Isle of Lewis in June 1993. Very fittingly, considering the yard's beginnings as a fishing-boat builder, *Delta Dawn III* was a wooden 40-footer with a beautifully varnished hull.

The decline in demand for fishing boats did not mark the end of boat building at Girvan. Indeed, nothing could be further from the truth as the yard's versatility has kept it busy building an assortment of steel vessels. Many of these are work-boats for the fish farming industry. One of the fish farm boats, *Grace*, delivered to Joseph Johnston Fish Farms of Scourie, Sutherland, in 1994, was the first boat built by Nobles using a computer-aided design system and was completed in only two and a half months. The yard has also built half a dozen small tugs.

Nobles' production of workboats for the aquaculture industry led in part to the securing of an order for a mussel dredger, *Gizzen Briggs*, which is registered as a fish-ing vessel with the number INS1040 and was delivered early in 2004. This vessel's owners, Highland Fresh Mussels Ltd, required a boat which could fish close inshore in shallow water and land to a tidal berth. As a result, they specified an extremely manoeuvrable, shallow-drafted boat with the highest possible load to hull immersion ratio. *Gizzen Briggs* was designed by naval architects A.G. Salmon & Co., well known for the design of steel and aluminium workboats. As her design was based on fish farm workboats it was logical that the contract to build her should be awarded to a yard that had experience of the construction of this type of vessel and Nobles took the opportunity to again build a boat which was at least registered as a fishing vessel.

Observers with fond memories of Nobles' ringers and 40-footers might dispute whether *Gizzen Briggs* should properly be regarded as a fishing boat. It is certainly correct that the work of a mussel dredger combines elements of the activities of both fishing boats and fish farm workboats. A mussel dredger is used to both harvest mar-ketable mussels and to gather seed mussels and relay these in selected beds. However, as *Gizzen Briggs* was completed, Nobles won an order for a steel beam trawler/stern trawler for Simon Jones of Exmouth in Devon. There is no doubt whatsoever that this was a fishing vessel and Nobles were once again building fishing craft. This boat, named *Emily J* (E123), was delivered early in 2005. Her overall length was 11.95m. If that is converted from metric measure into feet and inches we find that, in 2004, Nobles built another 40-footer.

From its beginnings on what Alexander Noble once described as a 'square of grass', Nobles' yard has developed and expanded. Back in the early days, the first building on the site was simply a 30ft-long shed to house equipment. This was extended to 70ft in 1947 to house additional machinery required due to increasing demands for building and repair work. The first slipway was built in 1948 and *Integrity* was the first vessel to use it. In 1950 a construction shed measuring 70ft by 60ft was built to avoid the rigours and handicaps of working in the open air. An engineering shop was erected in 1951. A small drawing office and general office were added in 1952 and later substantially extended. A second slipway was built in 1956. A large new slipway with an electric winch was commissioned in 1970, allowing Nobles to handle vessels of up to 250 tons displacement.

The new slip used to launch *Margarets* was constructed in 1986. This was a step that Nobles had had in mind for some time to allow them to repair larger vessels.

Margarets was built on the side of the shed where No.2 slip is located though, at the time, No.2 slip did not extend into the shed. It was obvious that the existing No.1 slip would not cope with her size and weight. Accordingly, the plans for the improvement of the yard were put into action and the improved slip was built on the site of No.1 slip. *Margarets* was moved across the shed on a carriage assembled below her and then out of the shed to be held in the open for a few days prior to launching. Despite her size, the operation went off without a hitch.

Maintenance and repair of vessels has, from the outset, been a significant part of the business of Alexander Noble & Sons Ltd. The yard has carried out a vast amount of repair work on fishing vessels, both boats built by Nobles themselves and vessels from other builders. Some of the repair jobs have been very substantial indeed. Things like the partial re-caulking of *Prospector*, the fitting of a new stem to *Aliped VIII*, the repair of damaged planking on *Ocean Gem* and the repair of collision damage to *Ribhinn Donn II* as a result of various misfortunes while fishing in the Minch are sizeable jobs but pale into insignificance beside some of the tasks undertaken by the yard's staff under the supervision of Peter Noble and which combine major repair work with what is virtually salvage work. This book records only a handful of many such instances.

Margarets dwarfing Nobles' yard. (Courtesy Alexander Noble & Sons Ltd, Girvan)

Little *Spes Bona* has twice suffered serious misfortunes in Ayr Harbour. The first occasion was on Christmas morning, 1955, when bad weather broke *Spes Bona's* moorings and drove her up the harbour under the railway bridge that spanned the River Ayr just upriver from the harbour. She became trapped under the bridge but was saved by Sandy Munro's *Incentive* (BA18) (built by Nobles of Fraserburgh). *Spes Bona's* seine net ropes were run along the quay to Incentive which pulled *Spes Bona* free and beached her in a corner of the north side of the harbour that dries out at low water. When Nobles inspected *Spes Bona*, they found she had been flooded and her interior had to be rebuilt.

The second occasion was in 1967 when *Spes Bona* was rammed by the 118ft steel side trawler *Duff Paton* (GW9). At one point it looked as if the little 40-footer would be cut in half by the much larger vessel. *Spes Bona* again flooded, sitting on the bottom of the harbour and had to be pumped out by the fire brigade. Nobles effected temporary repairs to the boat in the same corner of the north harbour where she had been beached before and she was then taken to Girvan to complete the repair work, which took nine weeks.

Another 40-footer, the *Audacious* (BA80), built by James N. Miller & Sons Ltd at St Monance, also flooded in the same part of Ayr Harbour as a result of one of the most bizarre misfortunes Peter Noble ever encountered. At the time, the River Ayr was in spate and carrying into the harbour a considerable assortment of rubbish and flotsam, which included an empty bottle, said to be a whisky bottle. This bottle drifted between *Audacious* and the quay and the impact of the boat being pushed against the quay didn't crush the bottle – incredibly it forced it right through a hull plank. Only then did the bottle break at the neck, leaving an inlet pipe for water to enter the hull. As the accident took place at the weekend, the boat was well flooded by the time it was discovered. Kenny Gibson of Nobles' *Wanderer* recollects a near repeat of this incident when a floating glass bottle was driven part of the way through *Wanderer's* planking.

One of Nobles' biggest accident repair jobs took place in 1951 and this was one which took the yard's staff into the realms of salvage as well as major repair. The vessel concerned was *Investor* (BA58), built by William Weatherhead at Cockenzie and owned by the McCrindle family of Maidens. In severe weather *Investor* had broken her moorings in Maidens Harbour and drifted across the harbour. When Nobles were called to the scene along with an insurance assessor from Glasgow, they found *Investor* lying against a stone wall where a burn enters the harbour. She had been pounding against the wall, badly damaging both the wall and her own port side. She had also been buried in sand up to her propeller shaft at the stern and to a depth of 1.5/2ft at the bow. At this point *Investor's* future was looking doubtful but Nobles set out to save her assisted by the McCrindles' crews and with the willing help of many other Maidens fishermen.

The first job was to dig the sand away from the boat. The bow was cleared first and a large oak beam eased under *Investor* to be used as a massive lever. This duly worked, raising the vessel's bow and the procedure was repeated at the stern. Nobles' workmen placed greased wooden sliding ways under *Investor*, creating a route by which she could be moved back to the water. A tractor was then used to move the boat along the ways, hauling through a big snatch block attached to the Maidens Rocks. The tractor moved *Investor* around 20ft at a time and by the end of the day she had been moved by 60/70ft. Work stopped as darkness fell and the tide began to rise. A gale sprang up that night but some of the boat's crew had taken the precaution of going aboard and, when *Investor* started to float, they started her engine and moved her to safety. She was thereafter moved to Girvan and slipped to complete the repairs. In an interesting coincidence, Nobles also had to rescue another Cockenzie-built boat from the same part of Maidens Harbour. This was the 40ft *Budding Rose* (BA313) and on that occasion the salvage proved rather more straightforward.

The most difficult of these operations took place in January 1968. A skipper once told the authors that 'the ring net fleet was blown out of the Minch at the start of 1968.' In some cases this was all too literally true as several ring net vessels were hurled ashore by hurricane force winds that hit the west of Scotland early on Monday 14 January. The casualties included Nobles' *Stormdrift*.

Stormdrift had, along with the Arbroath-built *Fair Wind* (BA177), been moored to a steamer buoy off the island of Kerrera after landing in Oban. The incredible force of the wind uprooted the anchor holding the buoy and shifted the buoy, the anchor and the two fishing vessels. The boats were thrown ashore on the calf of Kerrera.

Peter Noble received a phone call about *Stormdrift*'s plight later on the Monday, though it was Wednesday before Nobles' men could reach Oban due to the devastation caused by the storm and with fallen trees blocking the roads to the north. On arriving at Oban, Peter Noble met the unhappiest-looking group of skippers he had ever seen, all consumed with worry about their boats. *Jasmine* had come through the storm unscathed and took Noble's staff, Grieve Gemmell of *Stormdrift* and several other fishermen out to Kerrera to assess the state of the boats.

Fair Wind was still upright, though she was sitting on a ledge of rock disconcertingly close to the edge of a drop into the sea. *Stormdrift* was on her side, so far inland that she was touching the heather. One of her sides was visibly damaged, apparently having been repeatedly struck by a cathead on *Fair Wind*'s bow. Getting *Stormdrift* out of there was going to be a challenge.

Work started on the Thursday with *Jasmine* ferrying men and equipment to and from Oban. Once again Nobles used sliding wooden ways to form a route to move the boat back to the water and she had to be engineered on to the ways using jacks, mauls and wedges. As a safety precaution Peter Noble cut two eyebolts in *Stormdrift*'s keel and ran chains to the most immoveable-looking objects on the island. His concern was that once *Stormdrift* started to move on the ways, she would, in the absence of a restraint, slide away out of control, not that she had a clear path to the sea in any event. A substantial boulder blocked the way and it was far from clear how this obstacle would be surmounted. Willie Anderson of *Jasmine* took charge of this part of the operation. A cargo net procured in Oban was secured around the boulder and, when the tide was right, *Jasmine* used her ring net winch to drag the boulder out of *Stormdrift*'s path.

Stormdrift ashore on the Calf of Kerrera. *Fair Wind* is on the right of the picture. (Courtesy Alexander Noble & Sons Ltd, Girvan)

Another view of *Stormdrift* and *Fair Wind* aground on the Calf of Kerrera. (Courtesy Alexander Noble & Sons Ltd, Girvan)

Finally it was possible to begin moving *Stormdrift* along the greased timber ways. As the operation continued, one of the ways broke but, in a remarkable piece of good fortune, an old timber way even heavier than those in use was found behind the cottage on the island. The cottage was inhabited only in summer so there was no way of asking how a timber way came to be on the island but the obvious conclusion was that another vessel had previously been driven ashore in the same place and salvaged by the same means as those employed by Nobles.

Over a period of ten days, Noble's staff moved *Stormdrift* an estimated 70/75ft. They re-launched her in a flat calm at midnight on Sunday 27 January. Grieve Gemmell then started *Stormdrift*'s engine and took her into Oban.

Nobles' workmen were not yet finished as the following day they helped staff from Gerrard Brothers of Arbroath to put *Fair Wind* back in the water. *Fair Wind* had resisted all attempts to move her and her balancing act on the shelf of rock was a cause of much concern, the salvage team fearing that unless great care was taken with her she would topple over. It proved necessary to blast a way through the rock with explosives in order to return *Fair Wind* to the sea. After this had been done she was re-launched. She came perilously close to sinking immediately after that but was saved and later repaired. Meantime, *Stormdrift* returned to Girvan for repair, the biggest items being a new keel and several new planks.

Happily, at a time when the boat-building industry is in crisis and long-established fishing-boat builders have closed at an alarming rate, Nobles' yard continues to prosper and to build new boats, though fishing vessel orders are rare. In addition to building boats, the yard is kept busy with repair work on fishing vessels based on the west coast of Scotland, north-west England, Northern Ireland and the Isle of Man. Nobles can also attract repair work from much further afield – *L & T Britannia V* has on occasion come all the way from Cornwall to be overhauled by her builders who also fitted her three-quarter-length shelter in the winter of 1988/89. Another large job carried out to *L & T Britannia V* was the fitting of additional fuel tanks to allow her to take part in the drift net fishery for tuna, which involved her in steaming for as much as 3,000 miles in the course of a single trip.

L & T Britannia V back at her builders for overhaul. (Peter Drummond)

The yard's repair services are not confined to the fishing fleet. Nobles do maintenance work on pleasure vessels and carry out a substantial amount of repair work for the Royal National Lifeboat Institution. Lifeboat maintenance is usually to boats based on the west coast of Scotland but the yard has done work on lifeboats from the Scottish east coast, the Isle of Man, Northern Ireland and even the south of Ireland.

Also, despite the devastation of the British fishing industry by catch quotas, restrictions and decommissioning, a large number of fishing boats built by Nobles are still in commission and can be seen in harbours around the country. To anyone who knows anything about boats, a distinctive thistle emblem on a boat's bow means only one thing – built by Nobles of Girvan.

A TO Z OF FISHING BOATS BUILT BY NOBLES OF GIRVAN

There follows a comprehensive list of fishing vessels built by Alexander Noble & Sons Ltd. The authors have chosen to exclude mussel boats from this list and to treat them as non-fishing vessels for reasons of personal preference.

Under the heading 'Alterations' on each boat's page, we have not tried to record every change which was made to these boats but have instead confined ourselves to major modifications which significantly affect the external appearance of a vessel, though we will also include all changes of main engine known to us. The information, while believed to be correct, is not guaranteed to be absolutely accurate. The objective is to record for posterity what Nobles' fishing vessels were like and this book is not intended to be a substitute for any official source of information regarding fishing vessels.

The information contained in this book is, to the best of the authors' knowledge and belief, correct to 31 July 2009.

AJ BA844

Year Built:	2005
Yard No.:	130
Call Sign:	–
Hull:	Aluminium Catamaran

Principal dimensions in metres:

O/Length:	7.00
R/Length:	7.00
Breadth:	3.20
Depth:	0.70
Engine Make:	2 X Honda

HP:	150
Deck Layout:	Open deck with stern door
Type of Stern:	Transom
First Owners:	James T. Brawls, Port William

Vessel Re-named:	Re-numbered:	Year:
–	–	–

Alterations:	
Status:	Still fishing

ALIPED VIII BA155

Year Built:	1960
Yard No.:	37
Call Sign:	MEWF
Hull:	Wood

Principal dimensions in metres:

O/Length:	17.98
R/Length:	16.61
Breadth:	5.42
Depth:	2.68

Engine Make:	Kelvin T6
HP:	180
Deck Layout:	Open deck
Type of Stern:	Canoe
First Owners:	A. & T. McCrindle, Girvan

Vessel Re-named:	Re-numbered:	Year:
Aliped VIII	PL80	1986
Aliped VIII	N57	1986

Alterations:	310HP: Kelvin
Status:	Decommissioned 2002

ALIPED IX BA234

Year Built:	1964
Yard No.:	47
Call Sign:	MHPL
Hull:	Wood

AJ photographed when she was still the alu–cat. (Sam Henderson)

Aliped VIII when new. (Courtesy Alexander Noble & Sons Ltd, Girvan)

Aliped IX when new. (Courtesy Alexander Noble & Sons Ltd, Girvan)

Principal dimensions in metres:

O/Length:	17.98
R/Length:	16.76
Breadth:	5.58
Depth:	2.89

Engine Make:	Kelvin T6
HP:	180
Deck Layout:	Open deck
Type of Stern:	Canoe
First Owners:	A. & T. McCrindle, Girvan

Vessel Re-named:	**Re-numbered:**	**Year:**
Aliped IX	PD334	1982
Rona II	PD334	1983

Alterations:	310HP: Kelvin
	Gutting shelter

Status:	Vessel written off after being gutted by fire near Gairloch, 3 November 1992.

Opposite left: Alison Mary when new. (Courtesy Alexander Noble & Sons Ltd, Girvan/Lenny McLaughlin)

Opposite right: Alison Mary as *Investor* (BK107). (Courtesy David Linkie)

ALISON MARY N308

Year Built:	1979
Yard No.:	78
Call Sign:	2USG
Hull:	Wood

Principal dimensions in metres:

O/Length:	17.93
R/Length:	16.82
Breadth:	5.58
Depth:	2.45

Engine Make:	Gardner 8L3B
HP:	230
Deck Layout:	Open-deck Whaleback
Type of Stern:	Transom
First Owners:	I. Russel, Kilkeel

Vessel Re-named:	**Re-numbered:**	**Year:**
Investor	BK107	1985
Rose of Sharon V	LH250	2000

Alterations:	Port side shelter later extended to three-quarter-length shelter

Status:	Ran aground on rocks outside Seahouses Harbour in December, 2001. Vessel became total loss after being pounded by a succession of NNW gales and was broken up where she lay.

Alliance when new. (Courtesy Alexander Noble & Sons Ltd, Girvan)

ALLIANCE CN187

Year Built:	1974
Yard No.:	74
Call sign:	MQQK
Hull:	Wood

Principal dimensions in metres:

O/Length:	18.41
R/Length:	17.07
Breadth:	5.91
Depth:	2.51

Engine Make:	Caterpillar D343TA
HP:	365
Deck Layout:	Open deck
Type of Stern:	Canoe
First Owners:	W. & R. Gillies, Campbeltown

Vessel Re-named:	Re-numbered:	Year:
Alliance II	WD134	1990

Alterations:	–

Status:	Sank at Goat's Head near Glendore in thick fog and heavy seas, 2 May 1995. All crew picked up safely.

Opposite left: Annabelle. (Courtesy Mrs E. McIlwraith)

Opposite right: Annabelle seen when Lowestoft-registered, fitted with her new wheelhouse and fitted out for line fishing. (Courtesy Michael Craine)

ANNABELLE BA115

Year Built:	1950
Yard No.:	9
Call Sign:	GPFV
Hull:	Wood

Principal dimensions in metres:

O/Length:	12.16
R/Length:	11.40
Breadth:	4.30
Depth:	1.98
Engine Make:	Kelvin K3
HP:	66
Deck Layout:	Open deck
Type of Stern:	Canoe
First Owners:	W. McIlwraith, Ballantrae

Vessel Re-named:	Re-numbered:	Year:
Annabelle	A333	1979
Annabelle	LT308	1987

Alterations:	127HP: Gardner,
	127HP: Gardner (Second new engine)
	New wheelhouse

Status:	Ceased fishing 1996 and preserved on land at Cranworth near Dereham, Norfolk.

Above left: Aquila. (Courtesy Alexander Noble & Sons Ltd, Girvan)

Above right: Aquila as *Wanderer II* (CN142). (Courtesy John M. Addison)

AQUILA OB99

Year Built:	1972
Yard No.:	71
Call Sign:	MWHU
Hull:	Wood

Principal dimensions in metres:

O/Length:	16.76
R/Length:	15.69
Breadth:	5.27
Depth:	1.88

Engine Make:	Gardner 8L3B
HP:	230
Deck Layout:	Open deck
Type of Stern:	Cruiser
First Owners:	A. McLean, Dervaig, Isle of Mull

Vessel Re-named:	Re-numbered:	Year:
Beulah II	OB99	1988
Wanderer II	CN142	1993

Alterations:	328HP: Volvo Penta
	275HP: Caterpillar
	Gutting shelter

Status:	Still fishing

BOY JAMES BA52

Year Built:	1957
Yard No.:	27
Call Sign:	MXXW
Hull:	Wood

Principal dimensions in metres:

O/Length:	12.16
R/Length:	11.28
Breadth:	4.69
Depth:	1.74

Engine Make:	Kelvin K3
HP:	66
Deck Layout:	Open deck
Type of Stern:	Canoe
First Owners:	J. McMillan, Stranraer

Vessel Re-named:	Re-numbered:	Year:
Boy James	DO12	1963
Boy James	B8	1965
Boy James	CT72	1966
Boy James	B128	1973

Alterations:	110HP: Gardner
	127HP: Gardner

Status:	Ceased fishing 1999. Being converted to a house boat at Caernarvon.

Boy James. (Courtesy Alexander Noble & Sons Ltd, Girvan)

Above left: Boy Ken when new. (Courtesy Alexander Noble & Sons Ltd, Girvan)

Above right: Boy Ken as *Frey* (CT137). (Courtesy John M. Addison)

BOY KEN TT70

Year Built: 1972
Yard No.:   70
Call Sign: 2DFG
Hull: Wood

Principal dimensions in metres:
O/Length: 15.94
R/Length: 14.39
Breadth: 5.24
Depth: 1.95

Engine Make: Caterpillar D333TA
HP: 250
Deck Layout: Open deck
Type of Stern: Canoe
First Owners: J. Prentice, Tarbert & Partners

Vessel Re-named:	Re-numbered:	Year:
Frey	OB248	1973
Frey	CT137	1979

Alterations: 250HP: Caterpillar

Status: Still fishing

BRITANNIA BA130

Year Built:	1955
Yard No.:	21
Call Sign:	GTQC
Hull:	Wood

Principal dimensions in metres:

O/Length:	15.24
R/Length:	15.09
Breadth:	5.09
Depth:	1.98

Engine Make:	Gardner 5L3
HP:	95
Deck Layout:	Open deck
Type of Stern:	Cruiser
First Owners:	A. & T. Gibson, Dunure

Vessel Re-named:	**Re-numbered:**	**Year:**
–	–	–
Alterations:	–	

Status:	Converted to yacht 1965. Renamed *Craigweil*. Later renamed *Glory BV* and afterwards *Salmon Tails*.

Britannia. (Courtesy Scottish Fisheries Museum, Anstruther)

CALEDONIA TT17

Year Built: 1960
Yard No.:   35
Call Sign: MDHD
Hull: Wood

Principal dimensions in metres:
O/Length: 12.12
R/Length: 11.17
Breadth: 4.51
Depth: 1.90

Engine Make: Kelvin K3
HP: 66
Deck Layout: Open deck
Type of Stern: Canoe
First Owners: P. Brown & Partners, Tarbert

Vessel Re-named:	Re-numbered:	Year:
Threshlyn	PL98	1979
Threshlyn	N98	1984

Alterations: 112HP: Kelvin
                         New wheelhouse
                         New wheelhouse (Second new wheelhouse)

Status: Sold to owners in S. Ireland in 1985. No longer registered as a fishing
                         vessel..

Caledonia. (Courtesy
Alexander Noble &
Sons Ltd, Girvan)

Calina. (Courtesy John M. Addison)

CALINA SY47

Year Built:	1969
Yard No.:	64
Call Sign:	MOQP
Hull:	Wood

Principal dimensions in metres:

O/Length:	16.64
R/Length:	15.54
Breadth:	5.27
Depth:	1.89

Engine Make:	Gardner 6L3B
HP:	150
Deck Layout:	Open deck
Type of Stern:	Cruiser
First Owners:	A. Maclean & Partners, Ness, Isle of Lewis

Vessel Re-named:	**Re-numbered:**	**Year:**
–	–	–

Alterations:	Gutting shelter

Status:	Sprang leak and sank south-east of Stornoway, 19 April 2002.

CATHERINE R. ARMSTRONG BH44

Year Built: 1958
Yard No.:   30
Call Sign: MBHE
Hull: Wood

Principal dimensions in metres:

O/Length: 13.41
R/Length: 12.13
Breadth: 4.82
Depth: 1.98

Engine Make: Gardner 5L3
HP: 95
Deck Layout: Open deck
Type of Stern: Cruiser
First Owners: A. Armstrong, Amble

Vessel Re-named:	**Re-numbered:**	**Year:**
Border Lassie	BH44	1960

Alterations: 126HP: Gardner
New wheelhouse
Gutting shelter

Status: Still fishing

Above left: Catherine R. Armstrong. (Courtesy Alexander Noble & Sons Ltd, Girvan)

Above right: Catherine R. Armstrong as *Border Lassie* with a new wheelhouse and with her sides reinforced for scallop dredging. (Courtesy John M. Addison)

Crystal Sea.
(Courtesy
Alexander Noble
& Sons Ltd,
Girvan)

CRYSTAL SEA OB104

Year Built:	1963
Yard No.:	45
Call Sign:	MHLD
Hull:	Wood

Principal dimensions in metres:

O/Length:	18.32
R/Length:	16.95
Breadth:	5.58
Depth:	2.29

Engine Make:	Kelvin TS6
HP:	210
Deck Layout:	Open deck
Type of Stern:	Canoe
First Owners:	J. Manson, Mallaig

Vessel Re-named:	**Re-numbered:**	**Year:**
Crystal Sea	BA104	1973
Crystal Sea	CN314	1979
Crystal Sea II	CN314	1985
Crystal Sea II	N314	1989

Alterations:	310HP: Kelvin

Status:	Decommissioned 1996

DALRIADA TT77

Year Built:	1954
Yard No.:	20
Call Sign:	MLRA5
Hull:	Wood

Principal dimensions in metres:

O/Length:	12.16
R/Length:	10.58
Breadth:	4.45
Depth:	2.01

Engine Make:	Kelvin K3
HP:	66
Deck Layout:	Open deck
Type of Stern:	Canoe
First Owners:	R. A. Ross & partners, Tarbert

Vessel Re-named:	Re-numbered:	Year:
Dalriada	UL167	1978
Daystar	AH67	1986
Girl Margaret II	RO60	1991
Girl Margaret II	N914	1996

Alterations:	112HP: Kelvin
	Gutting shelter
	New wheelhouse
	Wheelhouse moved forward

Status:	Laid up in Ardglass and wheelhouse moved to forward position as part of intended conversion later aborted. Vessel scrapped 2008.

Right: Dawn Maid. (Courtesy Alexander Noble & Sons Ltd, Girvan)

Below: Dawn Maid registered as TN102 with a new wheelhouse and a gutting shelter. (Sam Henderson)

DAWN MAID CT99

Year Built:	1969
Yard No.:	62
Call Sign:	MOPZ
Hull:	Wood

Principal dimensions in metres:

O/Length:	16.51
R/Length:	15.60
Breadth:	5.29
Depth:	2.55

Engine Make:	Kelvin T8
HP:	240
Deck Layout:	Open deck
Type of Stern:	Cruiser
First Owners:	W. C. Waterson, Port Erin, Isle of Man

Vessel Re-named:	Re-numbered:	Year:
Dawn Maid	BA249	1992
Spes Bona IV	BA107	1995
Dawn Maid	TN102	2004

Alterations:	310HP: Gardner
	Gutting shelter
	New wheelhouse
	New gutting shelter
	Gutting shelter removed

Status:	Still fishing

Opposite left: Dalriada as *Daystar* (AH67). (Courtesy Scottish Fisheries Museum, Anstruther)

Opposite right: Dalriada as *Girl Margaret II* (N914). (Courtesy Sam Henderson)

Above left: Devorgilla. (Courtesy Alexander Noble & Sons Ltd, Girvan)

Above right: Devorgilla as *Harvester* (PD98). (Peter Drummond)

DEVORGILLA BA67

Year Built:	1978
Yard No.:	77
Call Sign:	2QPY
Hull:	Wood

Principal dimensions in metres:

O/Length:	21.09
R/Length:	19.54
Breadth:	6.71
Depth:	2.38

Engine Make:	Kelvin TBSC8
HP:	390
Deck Layout:	Open-deck Whaleback
Type of Stern:	Transom
First Owners:	D. Smith, Stranraer & partners

Vessel Re-named:	Re-numbered:	Year:
Devorgilla	LH217	1983
Harvester	PD98	1985
Good Hope	FR891	1996
Good Hope	B900	1998

Alterations:	495HP: Kelvin
	Three-quarter-length shelter

Status:	Decommissioned 2002

ELIZABETH CAMPBELL CN186

Year Built:	1950
Yard No.:	7
Call Sign:	MGTB
Hull:	Wood

Principal dimensions in metres:

O/Length:	16.76
R/Length:	15.76
Breadth:	5.18
Depth:	2.28

Engine Make:	Gleniffer DC6
HP:	120
Deck Layout:	Open deck
Type of Stern:	Canoe
First Owners:	J. Campbell, Carradale

Vessel Re-named:	**Re-numbered:**	**Year:**
Elizabeth Campbell	B58	1958
Elizabeth Campbell	SO283	1971
Elizabeth Campbell	B179	1973
Elizabeth Campbell	PL56	1975

Alterations:	120HP: Kelvin
Status:	Ceased fishing after severe fire off Peel, 11 February 1987. Plans for renovation of vessel as a houseboat came to nothing and she was broken up at Peel in 1998.

Elizabeth Campbell. (Courtesy Michael Craine)

Emily J. (Courtesy Alexander Noble & Sons Ltd, Girvan)

EMILY J. E123

Year Built:	2005
Yard No.:	129
Call Sign:	MGVR7
Hull:	Steel

Principal dimensions in metres:

O/Length:	11.95
R/Length:	11.41
Breadth:	5.50
Depth:	2.89

Engine Make:	Daewoo L126TIM
HP:	296
Deck Layout:	Open Deck
Type of Stern:	Transom
First Owners:	Simon Jones, Exmouth

Vessel Re-named:	**Re-numbered:**	**Year:**
–	–	–

Alterations:	296HP: Daewoo

Status:	Still fishing

EXCELLENT III OB89

Year Built:	1962
Yard No.:	42
Call Sign:	MFTU
Hull:	Wood

Principal dimensions in metres:

O/Length:	13.59
R/Length:	11.86
Breadth:	4.85
Depth:	1.98

Engine Make:	Gardner 6LX
HP:	110
Deck Layout:	Open deck
Type of Stern:	Cruiser
First Owners:	J. S. & A. Aitchison, Mallaig

Vessel Re-named:	**Re-numbered:**	**Year:**
Excellent III	SY289	1982

Alterations: –

Status: Sank in Brixham Harbour and afterwards broken up at Galmpton, 1997.

Above left: Excellent III. (Courtesy Alexander Noble & Sons Ltd, Girvan)

Above right: Excellent III in later life as SY289. (Courtesy John M. Addison)

Above left: Faithful approaching the south harbour entrance at Peterhead. (Courtesy Michael Forman)

Above right: Faithful outward bound to the drift net fishing. (Courtesy Michael Forman)

FAITHFUL PD307

Year Built:	1953
Yard No.:	18
Call Sign:	GRWS
Hull:	Wood

Principal dimensions in metres:

O/Length:	21.21
R/Length:	19.99
Breadth:	19.8
Depth:	9.40

Engine Make:	Kelvin KR6
HP:	132
Deck Layout:	Open deck
Type of Stern:	Cruiser
First Owners:	G. Forman & partners, Peterhead

Vessel Re-named:	**Re-numbered:**	**Year:**
Be Faithful	PD307	1971
Be Faithful	B10	1971

Alterations:	180HP: Kelvin
	New wheelhouse
	240HP: Kelvin
	430HP: Baudouin
	360HP: Caterpillar
	420HP: Caterpillar
	Gutting shelter

Status:	Decommissioned 1994

FENELLA ANN CT27

Year Built:	1960
Yard No.:	34
Call Sign:	MCUA
Hull:	Wood

Principal dimensions in metres:

O/Length:	15.30
R/Length:	14.57
Breadth:	5.33
Depth:	2.01

Engine Make:	2 x Kelvin K3 & K4
HP:	66 & 88
Deck Layout:	Open deck
Type of Stern:	Cruiser
First Owners:	J. Cunningham, Port Erin, Isle of Man

Vessel Re-named:	**Re-numbered:**	**Year:**
–	–	–

Alterations:	230HP: Gardner

Status:	Sank 9 November 2002 after striking rocks at southern part of Calf of Man, Isle of Man. *Fenella Ann*'s two-man crew were both picked up safely by *Heather Maid* (CT81).

Fenella Ann.
(Courtesy
Alexander Noble
& Sons Ltd,
Girvan)

GIRL MAUREEN BA128

Year Built: 1950
Yard No.:   10
Call Sign: GQVK
Hull: Wood

Principal dimensions in metres:

O/Length: 12.28
R/Length: 11.19
Breadth: 4.27
Depth: 1.98

Engine Make: Kelvin K3
HP: 66
Deck Layout: Open deck
Type of Stern: Canoe
First Owners: J. Lamb, Girvan

Vessel Re-named:	Re-numbered:	Year:
Girl Maureen	TT30	1970
Girl Maureen	LH148	1975
Morning Star	ME106	1977
Morning Star	OB426	1982
Girl Maureen	BA142	1993

Alterations: 66HP: Kelvin
127HP: Gardner

Status: Decommissioned 1994

Girl Maureen as *Morning Star* (ME106). (Courtesy Gloria Wilson)

Above left: Hercules II. (Courtesy Alexander Noble & Sons Ltd, Girvan)

Above right: Hercules II registered as LK438. By the time this picture was taken, her hull was protected against the rigours of scallop dredging. (Peter Drummond)

HERCULES II BA7

Year Built:	1968
Yard No.:	60
Call Sign:	2JXQ
Hull:	Wood

Principal dimensions in metres:

O/Length:	12.16
R/Length:	11.43
Breadth:	4.79
Depth:	2.10

Engine Make:	Kelvin R6
HP:	112
Deck Layout:	Open deck
Type of Stern:	Cruiser
First Owners:	J. & H. Edgar, Dunure

Vessel Re-named:	**Re-numbered:**	**Year:**
Hercules II	UL156	1977
Hercules II	LK438	1981

Alterations:	–

Status:	Decommissioned 1995

INTEGRITY BA335

Year Built:	1948
Yard No.:	4
Hull:	Wood

Principal dimensions in metres:

O/Length:	16.73
R/Length:	
Breadth:	5.21
Depth:	2.10

Engine Make:	Ruston & Hornsby 4VPHM
HP:	80
Deck Layout:	Open deck
Type of Stern:	Canoe
First Owners:	T. & W. Shields, Girvan

Vessel Re-named:	**Re-numbered:**	**Year:**
–	–	–

Alterations: –

Status: Ran aground on south side of Portpatrick Harbour, 22 November 1955. The Portpatrick lifeboat *Edward Z. Dresden* tried unsuccessfully to tow *Integrity* off the rocks. *Integrity*'s engine room flooded at midnight and her five-man crew was taken off safely by breeches buoy. *Integrity* later became a total loss.

Integrity. (Courtesy Alexander Noble & Sons Ltd, Girvan)

Above left: Islesman. (Courtesy Alexander Noble & Sons Ltd, Girvan)

Above right: Isleman as *Islander* (BA316) with her new wheelhouse. (Courtesy Sam Henderson)

ISLESMAN SY433

Year Built:	1967
Yard No.:	58
Call Sign:	MMIB
Hull:	Wood

Principal dimensions in metres:

O/Length:	16.10
R/Length:	15.54
Breadth:	5.27
Depth:	1.89

Engine Make:	Kelvin T6
HP:	180
Deck Layout:	Open deck
Type of Stern:	Cruiser
First Owners:	A. Maclean, Ness, Isle of Lewis

Vessel Re-named:	Re-numbered:	Year:
Islesman	BA141	1976
Boy Cameron II	BA141	1977
Boy Cameron II	INS314	1983
Islander	BA316	1990

Alterations:	New wheelhouse
	180HP: Doosan

Status:	Still fishing

Left: Janet Lang. (Courtesy James Noble)

Opposite left: Jasmine as CN118. By the time this picture was taken she had acquired a new wheelhouse and a gutting shelter on her port side. (Courtesy John M. Addison)

Opposite right: Jasmine seen after the end of her fishing career, her appearance probably enhanced by the removal of the gutting shelter. (Courtesy Michael Craine)

JANET LANG CN84

Year Built:	1949
Yard No.:	6
Call Sign:	MECE
Hull:	Wood

Principal dimensions in metres:

O/Length:	12.16
R/Length:	11.15
Breadth:	4.30
Depth:	2.01

Engine Make:	Kelvin K3
HP:	66
Deck Layout:	Open deck
Type of Stern:	Canoe
First Owners:	N. S. Lang, Campbeltown

Vessel Re-named:	Re-numbered:	Year:
Bessamarie	BA212	1963
Bessamarie	AH120	1966
New Era	OB90	1972
Morina	WK196	1975
Morina	KY58	1976
Lupin	BF231	1976
Lupin	FH139	1983

Alterations:	127HP: Gardner
	New wheelhouse

Status:	Decommissioned 1996

JASMINE BA55

Year Built:	1958
Yard No.:	28
Call Sign:	MYFP
Hull:	Wood

Principal dimensions in metres:

O/Length:	16.46
R/Length:	15.60
Breadth:	5.24
Depth:	1.90

Engine Make:	Gardner 6L3
HP:	114
Deck Layout:	Open deck
Type of Stern:	Cruiser
First Owners:	W. F. Anderson, Dunure

Vessel Re-named:	Re-numbered:	Year:
Jasmine	CN110	1973

Alterations:	200HP: Caterpillar
	New wheelhouse
	210HP: Gardner

Status:	Ceased fishing 1992. Then privately owned by Ken Watterson, Peel, Isle of Man, as research vessel for tracking sharks and pleasure trips. In 2003 sold to new owners in Poole for use as a diving boat.

Above left: Jasper. (Courtesy Alexander Noble & Sons Ltd, Girvan)

Above right: Jasper as *Santa Maria III* (CY38). (Courtesy John M. Addison)

JASPER SY379

Year Built:	1968
Yard No.:	59
Call Sign:	MZXW
Hull:	Wood

Principal dimensions in metres:

O/Length:	18.25
R/Length:	16.45
Breadth:	5.56
Depth:	2.35

Engine Make:	Gardner 8L3B
HP:	230
Deck Layout:	Open deck
Type of Stern:	Canoe
First Owners:	M. & E. McDonald, Scalpay, Isle of Harris

Vessel Re-named:	**Re-numbered:**	**Year:**
Santa Maria III	CY38	1971
Fair Morn	BA19	1988
Fair Morn	SY529	1991

Alterations:	Gutting shelter
Status:	Ceased fishing 1998. Saved from decommissioning and is now a pleasure boat lying in Loch Craignish.

JESSIE CN194

Year Built:	1950
Yard No.:	8
Call Sign:	MXVP
Hull:	Wood

Principal dimensions in metres:

O/Length:	12.16
R/Length:	11.48
Breadth:	4.30
Depth:	2.01

Engine Make:	Kelvin K3
HP:	66
Deck Layout:	Open deck
Type of Stern:	Canoe
First Owners:	J. Wareham, Campbeltown

Vessel Re-named:	**Re-numbered:**	**Year:**
Carra Rose	CN194	1976
Carra Rose	LN193	1982
Sundance	LT577	1987

Alterations:	84HP: Gardner
	127HP: Gardner
	New Wheelhouse

Status:	Decommissioned 1995

Above left: Jessie. (Courtesy W. Tudhope)

Above right: Jessie as Sundance (LT577). (Courtesy Stuart Emery)

JOB NO. 89 BA788

Year Built: 1993
Yard No.:   89
Call Sign: MAAW3
Hull: Wood

Principal dimensions in metres:
O/Length: 12.23
R/Length: 11.34
Breadth: 5.04
Depth: 2.20

Engine Make: Cummins N855M
HP: 224
Deck Layout: Open deck
Type of Stern: Transom
First Owners: N. McAulay, Isle of Lewis

Vessel Re-named:	**Re-numbered:**	**Year:**
Delta Dawn III	SY788	1993

Alterations: Gutting shelter

Status: Still fishing

Job No.89 as she is much better known – *Delta Dawn III* (SY788). (Courtesy John M. Addison)

Above left: L & T Britannia V. (Courtesy Alexander Noble & Sons Ltd, Girvan)

Above right: L & T Britannia V with her three-quarter-length shelter. (Sam Henderson)

L & T BRITANNIA V FH121

Year Built:	1986
Yard No.:	84
Call Sign:	GHLL
Hull:	Wood

Principal dimensions in metres:

O/Length:	15.45
R/Length:	14.17
Breadth:	5.64
Depth:	2.74

Engine Make:	Volvo Penta TAMD121C
HP:	347
Deck Layout:	Open-deck Whaleback
Type of Stern:	Transom
First Owners:	J.L. Leach & F.H. Turner, Mevagissey, Cornwall

Vessel Re-named:	**Re-numbered:**	**Year:**
Britannia V	FH121	2001

Alterations:	Three-quarter-length shelter
	380HP: Volvo Penta
	380HP: Volvo Penta

Status:	Still fishing

MAGDALENA CY203

Year Built: 1961
Yard No.:   39
Call Sign: MEPU
Hull: Wood

Principal dimensions in metres:
O/Length: 16.46
R/Length: 15.39
Breadth: 5.25
Depth: 1.86

Engine Make: Gardner 6L3
HP: 114
Deck Layout: Open deck
Type of Stern: Cruiser
First Owners: D. & J. Galbraith, Northbay, Barra

Vessel Re-named:	**Re-numbered:**	**Year:**
Comet	BF430	1966

Alterations: 172HP: Gardner
New wheelhouse
Gutting shelter

Status: Ceased fishing 2003. Vessel now pleasure boat moored at Port Ramsey, Lismore.

Above left: Magdalena. (Courtesy Alexander Noble & Sons Ltd, Girvan)

Above right: Magdalena as *Comet* beached for overhaul after cessation of fishing activities. (Courtesy M. Willis)

Magdalene Ann pictured in her later years by which time she had acquired her new wheelhouse and was fishing as a whelk potter. (Courtesy David Linkie)

MAGDALENE ANN CT33

Year Built:	1960
Yard No.:	36
Call Sign:	MDWU
Hull:	Wood

Principal dimensions in metres:

O/Length:	13.39
R/Length:	11.84
Breadth:	4.82
Depth:	1.98

Engine Make:	Gardner 5L3
HP:	95
Deck Layout:	Open deck
Type of Stern:	Cruiser
First Owners:	H. Goldsmith, Port St Mary, Isle of Man

Vessel Re-named:	**Re-numbered:**	**Year:**
Magdalene Ann	SH33	1983

Alterations:	150HP: Gardner
	New wheelhouse
	270HP: Volvo Penta
	150HP: Gardner

Status:	Still fishing

Margaret Stephen.
(Courtesy
Alexander Noble
& Sons Ltd,
Girvan)

MARGARET STEPHEN BA251

Year Built:	1947
Yard No.:	1
Call Sign:	MEWS
Hull:	Wood

Principal dimensions in metres:

O/Length:	12.16
R/Length:	11.30
Breadth:	4.26
Depth:	2.01

Engine Make:	Gleniffer DH3
HP:	36
Deck Layout:	Open deck
Type of Stern:	Canoe
First Owners:	P. Stephen, Girvan

Vessel Re-named:	**Re-numbered:**	**Year:**
Star of Hope II	CN262	1969
Wild Rover	BW21	1970
Wild Rover	SD70	1979

Alterations:	72HP: Gleniffer
	127HP: Gardner
	180HP: Gardner

Status:	Decommissioned 1993

MARGARETS LH232

Year Built:	1988
Yard No.:	86
Call Sign:	MJLF4
Hull:	Wood

Principal dimensions in metres:

O/Length:	21.00
R/Length:	19.10
Breadth:	7.05
Depth:	2.75

Engine Make:	Caterpillar D3412
HP:	540
Deck Layout:	Three-quarter-length shelter
Type of Stern:	Transom
First Owners:	D. Fairnie, Musselburgh

Vessel Re-named:	**Re-numbered:**	**Year:**
–	–	–

Alterations:	–

Status:	Still fishing

Margarets. (Sam Henderson)

MARIE BA211

Year Built:	1963
Yard No.:	46
Call Sign:	MHID
Hull:	Wood

Principal dimensions in metres:

O/Length:	17.95
R/Length:	16.58
Breadth:	5.55
Depth:	2.29

Engine Make:	Gardner 6L3B
HP:	150
Deck Layout:	Open deck
Type of Stern:	Canoe
First Owners:	H. & T.A. Anderson, Dunure

Vessel Re-named:	**Re-numbered:**	**Year:**
—	—	—

Alterations:	335HP: Caterpillar
	New wheelhouse
	Gutting shelter
	320HP: Volvo Penta

Status:	Ceased fishing 2006. Being converted to a floating electrical workshop.

Above left: Marie. (Courtesy Alexander Noble & Sons Ltd, Girvan)

Above right: Marie in later years with a new steel wheelhouse and gutting shelter. (Peter Drummond)

Marigold. (Courtesy Alexander Noble & Sons Ltd, Girvan)

MARIGOLD BA16

Year Built:	1956
Yard No.:	23
Call Sign:	MWMY
Hull:	Wood

Principal dimensions in metres:

O/Length:	11.37
R/Length:	10.70
Breadth:	4.57
Depth:	2.14

Engine Make:	Kelvin K3
HP:	66
Deck Layout:	Open deck
Type of Stern:	Canoe
First Owners:	J. & W. Gibson, Dunure

Vessel Re-named:	**Re-numbered:**	**Year:**
Marigold	OB32	1970
Marigold	PW73	1970
Marigold A	CO423	1978

Alterations:	66HP: Kelvin
	84HP: Gardner
	127HP: Gardner
	New wheelhouse
	New wheelhouse (Second new wheelhouse)
	127HP: Gardner (Second 6LXB Gardner fitted to vessel)

Status:	Ceased fishing late 1992. Laid up in Looe Harbour until July 1993 when sold to Scottish owners for use as a fish farm support vessel based at Fort William.

MAUREEN PATRICIA CT18

Year Built:	1970
Yard No.:	67
Call Sign:	MRIK
Hull:	Wood

Principal dimensions in metres:

O/Length:	14.00
R/Length:	12.08
Breadth:	5.02
Depth:	2.00

Engine Make:	Gardner 6L3B
HP:	150
Deck Layout:	Open deck
Type of Stern:	Cruiser
First Owners:	R.J. Watterson, Port Erin, Isle of Man

Vessel Re-named:	Re-numbered:	Year:
Maureen Patricia	OB582	1996
Maureen Patricia	CT18	1996
Maureen Patricia	N264	2003
Maureen Patricia	CT76	2006

Alterations:	–	

Status:	Still fishing

Above left: Maureen Patricia. (Courtesy Alexander Noble & Sons Ltd, Girvan)

Above right: Maureen Patricia seen later in her career. (Peter Drummond)

Michael J. (Courtesy Edward Sinclair)

MICHAEL J. CT9

Year Built:	1957
Yard No.:	25
Call Sign:	MFKJ7
Hull:	Wood

Principal dimensions in metres:

O/Length:	10.97
R/Length:	9.99
Breadth:	4.19
Depth:	1.61

Engine Make:	Kelvin K3
HP:	66
Deck Layout:	Open deck
Type of Stern:	Cruiser
First Owners:	J. Cunningham, Port Erin, Isle of Man

Vessel Re-named:	Re-numbered:	Year:
Michael J.	K926	1967
Michael J.	CT93	1968
Michael J.	B116	1973
Michael J.	BM138	1976
Michael J.	PL74	1977
Michael J.	K390	1982

Alterations:	108HP: Parsons Barracuda
	135HP: Ford

Status:	Returned to N. Ireland December 1984 but kept registration K390. Thereafter sold back to owners in Orkney. Still fishing from Kirkwall as K390.

MIZPAH BA11

Year Built:	1949
Yard No.:	5
Call Sign:	2DDJ
Hull:	Wood

Principal dimensions in metres:

O/Length:	12.16
R/Length:	10.67
Breadth:	4.27
Depth:	1.98

Engine Make:	Kelvin K3
HP:	66
Deck Layout:	Open deck
Type of Stern:	Canoe
First Owners:	A. & B. Dornan, Portpatrick

Vessel Re-named:	Re-numbered:	Year:
Mizpah	BA12	1978
Mizpah	N903	1996

Alterations:	90HP: Gardner
	New wheelhouse

Status:	Registry as British fishing vessel closed 4 July 2003. *Mizpah* thereafter based at Lough Swilly, S. Ireland, used for catching salmon until sold to Mike Williams of Baltimore, West Cork, S. Ireland in 2006. Boat to be restored to as close to her original condition as possible and used as pleasure vessel.

Mizpah. (Courtesy Scottish Marine Biological Association, Millport)

Above left: Moyallon leaving a rather gloomy Girvan Harbour on her trials. (Courtesy Alexander Noble & Sons Ltd, Girvan)

Above right: Moyallon amidst the scenic grandeur of the Scottish west coast. (Courtesy John M. Addison)

MOYALLON OB24

Year Built:	1985
Yard No.:	83
Call Sign:	MHFM3
Hull:	Wood

Principal dimensions in metres:

O/Length:	11.92
R/Length:	11.09
Breadth:	4.63
Depth:	2.22

Engine Make:	Gardner 6LXB
HP:	127
Deck Layout:	Open deck
Type of Stern:	Transom
First Owners:	N.M. Johnston, Mallaig

Vessel Re-named:	Re-numbered:	Year:
–	–	–

Alterations:	
	–

Status:	
	Still fishing

NEW DAWN BA19

Year Built:	1956
Yard No.:	24
Call Sign:	MXRC
Hull:	Wood

Principal dimensions in metres:

O/Length:	16.46
R/Length:	15.60
Breadth:	7.30
Depth:	6.60

Engine Make:	Gardner 6L3
HP:	114
Deck Layout:	Open deck
Type of Stern:	Cruiser
First Owners:	A. Munro & partners, Dunure

Vessel Re-named:	**Re-numbered:**	**Year:**
New Dawn	LH39	1968

Alterations:	110HP: Gardner

Status:	Now pleasure boat kept at moorings in River Medway, Kent.

Above left: New Dawn. (Courtesy Alexander Noble & Sons Ltd, Girvan)

Above right: New Dawn berthed in the River Medway after the end of her fishing career. (Courtesy Stuart Emery)

Above left: Ocean Gem. (Courtesy Alexander Noble & Sons Ltd, Girvan)

Above right: Ocean Gem seen in later life with a new wheelhouse and port side gutting shelter. (Peter Drummond)

OCEAN GEM BA265

Year Built:	1964
Yard No.:	49
Call Sign:	MIDD
Hull:	Wood

Principal dimensions in metres:

O/Length:	18.17
R/Length:	16.82
Breadth:	5.64
Depth:	2.32

Engine Make:	Gardner 8L3B
HP:	200
Deck Layout:	Open deck
Type of Stern:	Canoe
First Owners:	Mrs J. Andrew, Maidens

Vessel Re-named:	**Re-numbered:**	**Year:**
–	–	–

Alterations:	New wheelhouse
	230HP: Cummins
	Gutting shelter

Status:	Ceased fishing 2006. Being converted to a pleasure boat.

PATHFINDER BA252

Year Built: 1964
Yard No.:   48
Call Sign: MHXB
Hull: Wood

Principal dimensions in metres:
O/Length: 18.16
R/Length: 16.82
Breadth: 5.64
Depth: 2.31

Engine Make: Gardner 8L3B
HP: 200
Deck Layout: Open deck
Type of Stern: Canoe
First Owners: T.G. & D.H. Andrew, Maidens

Vessel Re-named:	Re-numbered:	Year:
Pathfinder	OB181	1973

Alterations: 230HP: Gardner
                       Gutting shelter (later removed)
                       300HP: Caterpillar

Status: Still fishing

Above left: Pathfinder. (Courtesy Alexander Noble & Sons Ltd, Girvan)

Above right: Pathfinder in later years – yet another Nobles' boat rigged out for the scallops. (Sam Henderson)

Above left: Prospector. (Courtesy Alexander Noble & Sons Ltd, Girvan)

Above right: Prospector seen in later life with a gutting shelter fitted. (Sam Henderson)

PROSPECTOR BA25

Year Built:	1973
Yard No.:	73
Call Sign:	2DAD
Hull:	Wood

Principal dimensions in metres:

O/Length:	16.95
R/Length:	15.50
Breadth:	5.23
Depth:	2.56

Engine Make:	Caterpillar D343TJ
HP:	300
Deck Layout:	Open deck
Type of Stern:	Transom
First Owners:	W.F. & I.W. Anderson, Dunure

Vessel Re-named:	**Re-numbered:**	**Year:**
Prospector	SH2	1983
Prospector	TT25	1991
Prospector	N1	2006

Alterations:	365HP: Volvo Penta
	Gutting shelter (later removed)

Status:	Still fishing

Right: Radiance seen in her later years with a gutting shelter fitted on her port side just visible behind her wheelhouse. (Peter Drummond)

Below right: Radiance when new. (Courtesy Alexander Noble & Sons Ltd, Girvan)

RADIANCE BA289

Year Built:	1966
Yard No.:	53
Call Sign:	MTTE
Hull:	Wood

Principal dimensions in metres:

O/Length:	12.01
R/Length:	11.19
Breadth:	4.67
Depth:	2.03

Engine Make:	Kelvin T3
HP:	90
Deck Layout:	Open deck
Type of Stern:	Transom
First Owners:	J. Johnston, Girvan

Vessel Re-named:	Re-numbered:	Year:
Radiance	CN132	1975
Radiance	TT97	1986
Radiance	N497	1997
Radiance	PL12	1998
Radiance	OB6	2005
Radiance	LK101	2007

Alterations:	180HP:Volvo Penta
	220HP:Volvo Penta
	320HP:Volvo Penta
	Gutting shelter (later removed)

Status:	Still fishing

RAMBLING ROSE N359

Year Built:	1981
Yard No.:	80
Call Sign:	MSDN7
Hull:	Wood

Principal dimensions in metres:

O/Length:	18.68
R/Length:	17.23
Breadth:	5.94
Depth:	2.77

Engine Make:	Caterpillar D3408 TA
HP:	365
Deck Layout:	Open deck Whaleback
Type of Stern:	Transom
First Owners:	C. McBride, Kilkeel

Vessel Re-named:	**Re-numbered:**	**Year:**
Rambling Rose	BCK21	1983

Alterations:	Three-quarter-length shelter
	402HP: Caterpillar

Status:	Still fishing

Above left: Rambling Rose. (Courtesy Alexander Noble & Sons Ltd, Girvan)

Above right: Rambling Rose registered BCK21 with her three-quarter-length shelter. (Courtesy John M. Addison)

Ranger.
(Courtesy
Alexander
Noble & Sons
Ltd, Girvan)

RANGER BA290

Year Built:	1966
Yard No.:	54
Call Sign:	MNTH
Hull:	Wood

Principal dimensions in metres:

O/Length:	16.52
R/Length:	15.61
Breadth:	5.22
Depth:	1.89

Engine Make:	Gardner 6L3B
HP:	150
Deck Layout:	Open deck
Type of Stern:	Cruiser
First Owners:	J. King, Kirkcudbright

Vessel Re-named:	**Re-numbered:**	**Year:**
Ranger	INS30	1971
Ranger	SY37	2002
Ranger A	SY37	2008

Alterations:	New wheelhouse
	Whaleback
	Gutting shelter

Status:	Still fishing

Opposite left: Rebena Belle. (Courtesy Alexander Noble & Sons Ltd, Girvan)

Opposite right: Rebena Belle registered N313 with her new wheelhouse and gutting shelter. (Sam Henderson)

REBENA BELLE CT63

Year Built:	1963
Yard No.:	44
Call Sign:	MGHB
Hull:	Wood

Principal dimensions in metres:

O/Length:	14.02
R/Length:	12.13
Breadth:	4.88
Depth:	1.98

Engine Make:	Gardner 6LX
HP:	110
Deck Layout:	Open deck
Type of Stern:	Cruiser
First Owners:	J.T. & A.Q. Cregeen, Port St Mary, Isle of Man

Vessel Re-named:	**Re-numbered:**	**Year:**
Rebena Belle	N313	1988

Alterations:	110HP: Cummins
	New wheelhouse
	Gutting shelter

Status:	Still fishing

Ribhinn Donn when new. (Courtesy Alexander Noble & Sons Ltd, Girvan)

Ribhinn Donn as *Ribhinn Bhan* seen in her last fishing days at the razor fish. (Sam Henderson)

RIBHINN DONN SY371

Year Built:	1966
Yard No.:	55
Call Sign:	MQZE
Hull:	Wood

Principal dimensions in metres:

O/Length:	17.18
R/Length:	15.73
Breadth:	5.24
Depth:	2.33

Engine Make:	Gardner 6L3B
HP:	150
Deck Layout:	Open deck
Type of Stern:	Canoe
First Owners:	J. & H. McLeod, Scalpay, Isle of Harris

Vessel Re-named:	Re-numbered:	Year:
Ribhinn Bhan	SY371	1973
Ribhinn Bhan	PL89	1986
Ribhinn Bhan	B23	1989

Alterations:	195HP: Cummins
	Gutting shelter

Status:	Ceased to be registered as a British fishing vessel 2004. *Ribhinn Bhan* was thereafter based at Tarbert, used for catching razor fish until sold to Mike Williams of Baltimore, West Cork, S. Ireland in 2006. Boat to be restored to as close to her original condition as possible and used as pleasure vessel.

RIBHINN DONN II SY141

Year Built:	1973
Yard No.:	72
Call Sign:	GSOA
Hull:	Wood

Principal dimensions in metres:

O/Length:	19.30
R/Length:	18.01
Breadth:	5.91
Depth:	2.67

Engine Make:	Gardner 8L3B
HP:	230
Deck Layout:	Open deck
Type of Stern:	Canoe
First Owners:	J. & A. McLeod, Scalpay, Isle of Harris

Vessel Re-named:	**Re-numbered:**	**Year:**
Ribhinn Donn II	B140	1989

Alterations:	230HP: Caterpillar
	Gutting shelter

Status:	Still fishing

Ribhinn Donn II.
(Sam Henderson)

Rose of Sharon M.
(Courtesy Alexander
Noble & Sons Ltd, Girvan)

ROSE OF SHARON M N349

Year Built:	1979
Yard No.:	79
Call Sign:	MAHB2
Hull:	Wood

Principal dimensions in metres:

O/Length:	18.79
R/Length:	16.48
Breadth:	5.94
Depth:	3.58

Engine Make:	Caterpillar D3408TA
HP:	365
Deck Layout:	Open-deck Whaleback
Type of Stern:	Transom
First Owners:	W. McBride, Kilkeel

Vessel Re-named:	**Re-numbered:**	**Year:**
Rose of Sharon M	BH7	1983
Provider A	BH7	1983
Provider A	AH27	1988

Alterations:	Three-quarter-length shelter

Status:	Began taking in water when prawn trawling in North Sea. Taken in tow by *True Vine* (KY7) but sank 8 miles off Amble, 6 December 1991. All crew picked up safely.

Rosemary Ann.
(Courtesy Alexander
Noble & Sons Ltd,
Girvan)

ROSEMARY ANN BA279

Year Built: 1965
Yard No.: 51
Call Sign: MIMZ
Hull: Wood

Principal dimensions in metres:
O/Length: 13.72
R/Length: 13.01
Breadth: 4.72
Depth: 1.98

Engine Make: Kelvin R6
HP: 112
Deck Layout: Open deck
Type of Stern: Cruiser
First Owners: T. McCrindle, Girvan

Vessel Re-named:	Re-numbered:	Year:
Rosemary Ann	B279	1992

Alterations: 150HP: Gardner
Gutting shelter

Status: Still fishing

SAFFRON BA182

Year Built:	1951
Yard No.:	12
Call Sign:	MMTQ
Hull:	Wood

Principal dimensions in metres:

O/Length:	17.67
R/Length:	16.31
Breadth:	5.49
Depth:	2.07

Engine Make:	Gardner 8L3
HP:	152
Deck Layout:	Open deck
Type of Stern:	Canoe
First Owners:	S.T. McCrindle & partners, Maidens

Vessel Re-named:	**Re-numbered:**	**Year:**
Maid of Honour	CN120	1973
Maid of Honour	LH120	1977
Saffron	LH120	1984
Utopia	B563	1989

Alterations:	185HP: Volvo Penta

Status:	Decommissioned 1996

Saffron. (Courtesy Michael Craine)

SAPPHIRE BA174

Year Built:	1962
Yard No.:	40
Call Sign:	MGIJ
Hull:	Wood

Principal dimensions in metres:

O/Length:	17.88
R/Length:	16.40
Breadth:	5.56
Depth:	2.22

Engine Make:	Gardner 8L3B
HP:	230
Deck Layout:	Open deck
Type of Stern:	Canoe
First Owners:	T.A.S. & W.A. McCrindle, Maidens

Vessel Re-named:	**Re-numbered:**	**Year:**
Sapphire	CN174	1976
Sapphire	N64	1986

Alterations:	230HP: Gardner

Status:	Decommissioned 1996

Sapphire. (Courtesy Alexander Noble & Sons Ltd, Girvan)

Above left: Seascan ready for launching. (Courtesy Alexander Noble & Sons Ltd, Girvan)

Above right: Seascan with her new wheelhouse. (Sam Henderson)

SEASCAN WA16

Year Built:	1962
Yard No.:	43
Call Sign:	GLQE
Hull:	Wood

Principal dimensions in metres:

O/Length:	12.6
R/Length:	11.9
Breadth:	4.8
Depth:	1.9

Engine Make:	Gardner 6LX
HP:	110
Deck Layout:	Open deck
Type of Stern:	Cruiser
First Owners:	UK Atomic Energy Authority

Vessel Re-named:	**Re-numbered:**	**Year:**
–	–	–

Alterations:	New wheelhouse
	127HP: Gardner

Status:	Vessel was registered as a fishing boat but used to take samples of marine life to check for any traces of radioactive contamination from nuclear power facility at Sellafield, Cumbria. In 2007 she was sold to Jim Barlow of Fleetwood for use as a pleasure boat.

Seeker. (Courtesy Alexander Noble & Sons Ltd, Girvan)

SEEKER CN49

Year Built:	1969
Yard No.:	63
Call Sign:	MORD
Hull:	Wood

Principal dimensions in metres:

O/Length:	12.14
R/Length:	11.40
Breadth:	4.83
Depth:	2.16

Engine Make:	Kelvin R6
HP:	112
Deck Layout:	Open deck
Type of Stern:	Cruiser
First Owners:	P.J. Campbell, Carradale

Vessel Re-named:	Re-numbered:	Year:
Brighter Morn	CN151	1975
Seeker	CN151	1976
Sweet Promise	SS95	1979
Ocean Harvest	BH46	1983
Seeker	CN694	1999

Alterations:	170HP: Gardner
	240HP: Volvo Penta
	Gutting shelter

Status:	Sank near the Shiant Islands, 17 miles north of Stornoway, July 2004.

SELINA II BA333

Year Built:	1948
Yard No.:	2
Call Sign:	–
Hull:	Wood

Principal dimensions in metres:

O/Length:	12.12
R/Length:	11.25
Breadth:	4.30
Depth:	1.95

Engine Make:	Kelvin K2
HP:	44
Deck Layout:	Open deck
Type of Stern:	Canoe
First Owners:	D. McCrindle, Girvan

Vessel Re-named:	**Re-numbered:**	**Year:**
Reaper	BF396	1953
Reaper	FR17	1968
Reaper	WK87	1972

Alterations:	140HP: Volvo Penta

Status: Written off after severe fire believed to have been started by a faulty cabin heater May 1976. Burned out in Rispond Harbour (Loch Eriboll) when the crew were at home in Caithness due to bad weather. The burnt-out hull was towed to Talamine (Kyle of Tongue) where she still lies today.

Selina II as *Reaper* WK87. (Courtesy Harry Henderson)

SILVER CHORD BA62

Year Built:	1958
Yard No.:	29
Call Sign:	MYJZ
Hull:	Wood

Principal dimensions in metres:

O/Length:	12.76
R/Length:	11.22
Breadth:	4.85
Depth:	2.00

Engine Make:	Gardner 4L3
HP:	76
Deck Layout:	Open deck
Type of Stern:	Cruiser
First Owners:	A. Farquhar & J. Geddes, Girvan

Vessel Re-named:	**Re-numbered:**	**Year:**
Stroma	BA62	1976

Alterations:	Gutting shelter
	New wheelhouse

Status:	Decommissioned 1995

Above left: Silver Chord. (Courtesy Alexander Noble & Sons Ltd, Girvan)

Above right: Silver Chord as Stroma. (Peter Drummond)

Above left: Silver Quest. (Courtesy Alexander Noble & Sons Ltd, Girvan)

Above right: Silver Quest as DO76. (Sam Henderson)

SILVER QUEST BA302

Year Built:	1967
Yard No.:	57
Call Sign:	MWKA
Hull:	Wood

Principal dimensions in metres:

O/Length:	17.25
R/Length:	15.33
Breadth:	5.29
Depth:	1.74

Engine Make:	Gardner 6L3B
HP:	150
Deck Layout:	Open deck
Type of Stern:	Canoe
First Owners:	R. & T. McCutcheon & T. Hay, Dunure

Vessel Re-named:	**Re-numbered:**	**Year:**
Silver Quest	DO76	1979

Alterations:	–

Status:	Ceased fishing 2003 and being converted to charter vessel at Maryport.

SILVERY SEA OB156

Year Built:	1965
Yard No.:	50
Call Sign:	MIEK
Hull:	Wood

Principal dimensions in metres:

O/Length:	18.47
R/Length:	17.07
Breadth:	5.58
Depth:	2.28

Engine Make:	Kelvin T8
HP:	240
Deck Layout:	Open deck
Type of Stern:	Canoe
First Owners:	A.J. Manson & J.T. Manson, Mallaig

Vessel Re-named:	**Re-numbered:**	**Year:**
Silvery Sea	CY105	1974
Regina Maris	CY105	1974

Alterations:	310HP: Kelvin
	Gutting shelter

Status:	Decommissioned 1996

Silvery Sea. (Courtesy Alexander Noble & Sons Ltd, Girvan)

Spes Bona.
(Courtesy Donald Gibson)

SPES BONA BA17

Year Built: 1955
Yard No.:   22
Call Sign:
Hull: Wood

Principal dimensions in metres:

O/Length: 12.16
R/Length: 10.48
Breadth: 4.48
Depth: 1.89

Engine Make:	Kelvin K3	
HP:	66	
Deck Layout:	Open deck	
Type of Stern:	Canoe	
First Owners:	R. W. & T. Gibson, Dunure	

Vessel Re-named:	**Re-numbered:**	**Year:**
Spes Bona	BCK17	1971
Spes Bona	OB310	1979

Alterations:	84HP: Gardner
	New wheelhouse

Status:	Vessel sank near Crinan, June 1981

SPES BONA II BA107

Year Built:	1971
Yard No.:	69
Call Sign:	2MMM
Hull:	Wood

Principal dimensions in metres:

O/Length:	12.12
R/Length:	11.29
Breadth:	4.82
Depth:	2.13

Engine Make:	Caterpillar D333
HP:	200
Deck Layout:	Open deck
Type of Stern:	Transom
First Owners:	R. W. Gibson & D.M.A. Gibson, Dunure

Vessel Re-named:	**Re-numbered:**	**Year:**
Spes Nova	CN77	1991

Alterations:	Gutting shelter
	210HP: Caterpillar

Status:	Sank 6 miles north east of Portree, 30 November 2007. All crew picked up safely by *Arnborg* (LK172).

Spes Bona II when new. (Courtesy Alexander Noble & Sons Ltd, Girvan)

Spes Bona II as *Spes Nova* (CN77). (Sam Henderson)

SPINDRIFT BA220

Year Built:	1974
Yard No.:	75
Call Sign:	2HEV
Hull:	Wood

Principal dimensions in metres:

O/Length:	16.98
R/Length:	15.48
Breadth:	5.46
Depth:	2.04

Engine Make:	Scania Vabis DSI140M1
HP:	270
Deck Layout:	Open deck Whaleback
Type of Stern:	Transom
First Owners:	D. McLean, Maidens

Vessel Re-named:	**Re-numbered:**	**Year:**
Sharon Rose	SY190	1999

Alterations:	328HP: Volvo Penta
	Gutting shelter

Status:	Still fishing

Above left: Spindrift when new. (Courtesy Alexander Noble & Sons Ltd, Girvan)

Above right: Spindrift seen with her gutting shelter. (Peter Drummond)

Stjernen. (Sam Henderson)

STJERNEN WA31

Year Built:	1959
Yard No.:	31
Call Sign:	MBIU
Hull:	Wood

Principal dimensions in metres:

O/Length:	12.13
R/Length:	10.64
Breadth:	4.58
Depth:	1.89

Engine Make:	Kelvin K3
HP:	66
Deck Layout:	Open deck
Type of Stern:	Canoe
First Owners:	E.L. Jensen and O.A. Bergman, Whitehaven

Vessel Re-named:	Re-numbered:	Year:
—	—	—

Alterations:	88HP: Volvo Penta
	New wheelhouse

Status:	Still fishing

STORMDRIFT BA187

Year Built:	1962
Yard No.:	41
Call Sign:	MFBU
Hull:	Wood

Principal dimensions in metres:

O/Length:	17.97
R/Length:	16.13
Breadth:	5.55
Depth:	2.29

Engine Make:	Gardner 6L3B
HP:	150
Deck Layout:	Open deck
Type of Stern:	Canoe
First Owners:	G. & J. Gemmell, Dunure

Vessel Re-named:	**Re-numbered:**	**Year:**
Stormdrift	CN368	1994

Alterations:	335HP: Caterpillar
	New wheelhouse
	Gutting shelter
	360HP: Cummins

Status:	Ceased fishing 2004. Sold to owners in S. Ireland for conversion to a houseboat.

Above left: Stormdrift when new. (Courtesy Alexander Noble & Sons Ltd, Girvan)

Above right: Stormdrift seen with her new wheelhouse. (Peter Drummond)

Summer Morn. (Courtesy John M Addison)

SUMMER MORN B78

Year Built: 1957
Yard No.:   26
Call Sign: MXVD
Hull: Wood

Principal dimensions in metres:
O/Length: 18.17
R/Length: 17.28
Breadth: 5.52
Depth: 1.92

Engine Make: Gardner 8L3
HP: 152
Deck Layout: Open deck
Type of Stern: Cruiser
First Owners: J.H. Cully & partners, Portavogie

Vessel Re-named:	Re-numbered:	Year:
—	—	—

Alterations: 230HP: Gardner

Status: Decommissioned 1994

SYRINEN WA6

Year Built:	1959
Yard No.:	33
Call Sign:	MCIJ
Hull:	Wood

Principal dimensions in metres:

O/Length:	12.14
R/Length:	10.64
Breadth:	4.57
Depth:	1.89

Engine Make:	Kelvin K3
HP:	66
Deck Layout:	Open deck
Type of Stern:	Canoe
First Owners:	P. Pederson & P.A. Haraldsen, Whitehaven

Vessel Re-named:	Re-numbered:	Year:
Lorraine	WA6	1961
Syrinen	WA6	1971
Syrinen	BS2	1990

Alterations:	112HP: Kelvin
	New wheelhouse
	Gutting shelter
	110HP: Gardner

Status:	Still fishing

TRUE TOKEN B600

Year Built:	1965
Yard No.:	52
Call Sign:	MKNH
Hull:	Wood

Principal dimensions in metres:

O/Length:	18.14
R/Length:	17.26
Breadth:	5.63
Depth:	2.34

Engine Make:	Gardner 8L3B
HP:	200
Deck Layout:	Open deck
Type of Stern:	Canoe
First Owners:	D. & H. Adair, Portavogie

Vessel Re-named:	**Re-numbered:**	**Year:**
True Token	CN298	1981

Alterations:	300HP: Cummins
	New wheelhouse
	Gutting shelter

Status:	Still fishing

Left: Syrinen. (Sam Henderson)

Below left: True Token. (Courtesy Alexander Noble & Sons Ltd, Girvan)

Below right: True Token registered CN298. No longer a ringer/trawler, she is now a scalloper/trawler. (Peter Drummond)

Valaura. (Courtesy John M. Addison)

VALAURA BA256

Year Built:	1987
Yard No.:	85
Call Sign:	MCWL5
Hull:	Steel

Principal dimensions in metres:

O/Length:	13.40
R/Length:	11.89
Breadth:	5.40
Depth:	2.20

Engine Make:	Gardner 6LYT
HP:	260
Deck Layout:	Three-quarter-length shelter
Type of Stern:	Transom
First Owners:	D. & E. McCrindle, Girvan

Vessel Re-named:	**Re-numbered:**	**Year:**
–	–	–

Alterations:	Three-quarter-length shelter removed
	250HP: Gardner

Status:	Still fishing

VIGILANT SY28

Year Built: 1968
Yard No.: 61
Call Sign: MZWN
Hull: Wood

Principal dimensions in metres:
O/Length: 19.17
R/Length: 17.94
Breadth: 5.94
Depth: 2.74

Engine Make: Kelvin T8
HP: 240
Deck Layout: Open deck
Type of Stern: Canoe
First Owners: D.W. MacLeod, Scalpay, Isle of Harris

Vessel Re-named:	**Re-numbered:**	**Year:**
Vigilant	UL55	1977

Alterations: 320HP: Kelvin
Gutting shelter
410HP: Kelvin

Status: Still fishing

Above left: Vigilant. (Courtesy Alexander Noble & Sons Ltd, Girvan)

Above right: Vigilant registered as UL55. (Courtesy Iain Mciver)

VILLAGE BELLE IV TT74

Year Built:	1970
Yard No.:	65
Call Sign:	MOYJ
Hull:	Wood

Principal dimensions in metres:

O/Length:	18.29
R/Length:	17.04
Breadth:	5.82
Depth:	2.52

Engine Make:	Kelvin T8
HP:	240
Deck Layout:	Open deck
Type of Stern:	Canoe
First Owners:	W. Jackson & partners, Tarbert

Vessel Re-named:	Re-numbered:	Year:
–	–	–

Alterations:	375HP: Kelvin
	Gutting shelter (later removed)
	375HP: Cummins

Status:	Still fishing

Above left: Village Belle IV as a handsome new ringer. (Courtesy Alexander Noble & Sons Ltd, Girvan)

Above right: Village Belle IV in later years as a prawn trawler. (Sam Henderson)

Village Maid.
(Courtesy
Alexander Noble &
Sons Ltd, Girvan)

VILLAGE MAID SY63

Year Built:	1970
Yard No.:	66
Call Sign:	MSAJ
Hull:	Wood

Principal dimensions in metres:

O/Length:	18.27
R/Length:	16.99
Breadth:	5.82
Depth:	2.55

Engine Make:	Gardner 8L3B
HP:	230
Deck Layout:	Open deck
Type of Stern:	Canoe
First Owners:	K. McKay & partners, Scalpay, Isle of Harris

Vessel Re-named:	**Re-numbered:**	**Year:**
Silver Dawn	CN199	1985
Silver Dawn	OB333	1990

Alterations:	350HP: Cummins
	Gutting shelter

Status:	Still fishing

Village Maid as *Silver Dawn* (OB333). (Sam Henderson)

Village Maid II. (Courtesy Scottish Fisheries Museum, Anstruther)

VILLAGE MAID II TT25

Year Built:	1961
Yard No.:	38
Call Sign:	MEGV
Hull:	Wood

Principal dimensions in metres:

O/Length:	17.85
R/Length:	16.45
Breadth:	5.55
Depth:	2.27

Engine Make:	Gardner 8L3
HP:	152
Deck Layout:	Open deck
Type of Stern:	Canoe
First Owners:	W. & N.K. Jackson, Tarbert

Vessel Re-named:	**Re-numbered:**	**Year:**
Village Maid II	OB154	1989

Alterations:	240HP: Kelvin
	270HP: Volvo Penta
	New wheelhouse

Status:	Decommissioned 1994

WANDERER BA298

Year Built:	1967
Yard No.:	56
Call Sign:	MUMG
Hull:	Wood

Principal dimensions in metres:

O/Length:	12.16
R/Length:	11.37
Breadth:	4.79
Depth:	1.98

Engine Make:	Kelvin R6
HP:	112
Deck Layout:	Open deck

Wanderer. (Courtesy Alexander Noble & Sons Ltd, Girvan)

Wanderer slipped for overhaul when registered A279. (Courtesy James A. Pottinger)

| Type of Stern: | Cruiser |
| First Owners: | T.K & D. Gibson, Dunure |

Vessel Re-named:	Re-numbered:	Year:
Wanderer	PD181	1977
Wanderer	WK501	1978
Wanderer	A279	1979
Wanderer	CN79	1986

| Alterations: | 180HP: Caterpillar |
| | 270HP: Cummins |

| Status: | Decommissioned 1993 |

WANDERER II BA76

Year Built:	1975
Yard No.:	76
Call Sign:	2THK
Hull:	Wood

Principal dimensions in metres:

O/Length:	21.07
R/Length:	19.51
Breadth:	6.56
Depth:	2.44
Engine Make:	Kelvin TBSC8
HP:	450
Deck Layout:	Open deck Whaleback
Type of Stern:	Transom
First Owners:	D. & K. Gibson, Dunure & partners

Vessel Re-named:	Re-numbered:	Year:
Freedom IV	LH371	1983
Sunrise	LK76	1984
Astral	INS116	1987

Alterations:	Gutting shelter
	Three-quarter-length shelter
	450HP: Kelvin

| Status: | Decommissioned 2002 |

Wanderer II. (Courtesy Alexander Noble & Sons Ltd, Girvan)

Above:Wanderer II as *Astral* INS 116. (Courtesy John M. Addison)

Opposite:Westerlea. (Courtesy Alexander Noble & Sons Ltd, Girvan)

WESTERLEA OB93

Year Built: 1971
Yard No.:   68
Call Sign: MUHB
Hull: Wood

Principal dimensions in metres:

O/Length: 19.26
R/Length: 17.95
Breadth: 5.94
Depth: 2.07

Engine Make: Kelvin T8
HP: 240
Deck Layout: Open deck
Type of Stern: Canoe
First Owners: J. & P. MacLean, Mallaig

Vessel Re-named:	Re-numbered:	Year:
Huntress	BA93	1979

Alterations: –

Status: Decommissioned 2002

APPENDIX 1

BUILDING A NOBLES CLASSIC

Skipper
David Smith's
Devorgilla
(BA67) begins
to take shape
as the frames
are erected.
(Courtesy
Alexander
Noble & Sons
Ltd, Girvan)

Planking just
above the keel.
(Courtesy
Alexander
Noble & Sons
Ltd, Girvan)

Planking continues. (Courtesy Alexander Noble & Sons Ltd, Girvan)

A view of the deck. (Courtesy Alexander Noble & Sons Ltd, Girvan)

The wheelhouse is craned aboard. (Courtesy Alexander Noble & Sons Ltd, Girvan)

The propeller. (Courtesy Alexander Noble & Sons Ltd, Girvan)

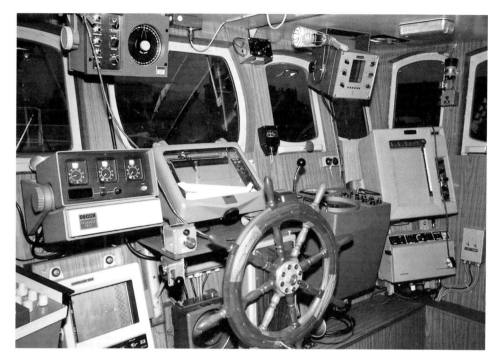

Inside the fitted out wheelhouse. (Courtesy Alexander Noble & Sons Ltd, Girvan)

The whaleback is lifted aboard. (Courtesy Alexander Noble & Sons Ltd, Girvan)

The winch newly lifted aboard. (Courtesy Alexander Noble & Sons Ltd, Girvan)

The finished article ready for launch. (Courtesy Alexander Noble & Sons Ltd, Girvan)

APPENDIX 2

PHOTO MISCELLANY

Ringers in Portpatrick (1). It's August 1962 and the ring net fleet is clustered into Portpatrick Harbour to land herring caught at the Isle of Man and bringing the little village harbour to life in a way that delighted summer visitors and which will never be seen again. Nobles' boats are represented by *Britannia* (BA130) landing on the right while brand new *Stormdrift* (BA187) is sticking her stern into the left of the picture. The boat in the centre of the shot is *Heritage* (BA74), which came from the other Nobles – James Noble of Fraserburgh. (The late Mrs M.J. M. Drummond)

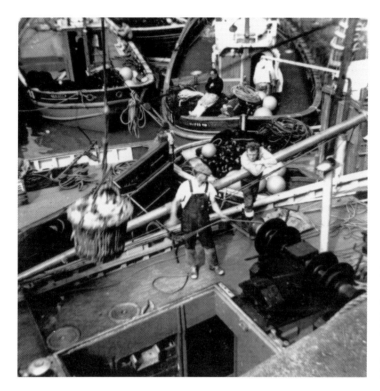

Ringers in Portpatrick (2). Another cluster of ringers in Portpatrick in August 1962, Nobles' *Aliped VIII* (BA155) is seen from aft. (The late Mrs M.J.M. Drummond)

Ringers in the Maidens. It's August 1965 and Maidens still has its renowned fleet of ringers. Nobles' boats are represented by *Sapphire* (BA174) lying outside of the Fairlie-built *Silver Lining* (BA158) (The late Mrs M.J.M. Drummond)

Ring net days (1). *Village Maid* (SY63). (Courtesy Alexander Noble & Sons Ltd, Girvan)

Ring net days (2). *Ribhinn Donn* (SY371). (Courtesy Alexander Noble & Sons Ltd, Girvan)

Opposite above: Launches (1). *Vigilant* (SY28) leaving the shed. (Courtesy Alexander Noble & Sons Ltd, Girvan)

Opposite below: Launches (2). *Rosemary Ann* (BA279) sliding down the slip. (Courtesy Alexander Noble & Sons Ltd, Girvan)

Launches (3). *Wanderer* (BA298) takes to the water for the first time. (Courtesy Alexander Noble & Sons Ltd, Girvan)

Launch ladies (1). Left to right: Annette, Kathryn and Shirley McLean ready to help launch Dad's (Skipper Donald McLean's) *Spindrift* (BA220). (Courtesy Alexander Noble & Sons Ltd, Girvan)

Above: Launch ladies (2). Hazel Crossan, sister of Skipper Ian Anderson, shatters the traditional champagne bottle on the bow of *Prospector* (BA25). (Courtesy Alexander Noble & Sons Ltd, Girvan)

Left: Launch ladies (3). Doreen Gemmell, daughter of Skipper Grieve Gemmell, does the honours for *Stormdrift* (BA187) while Mum (Mrs Margaret Gemmell) keeps an eye on the proceedings. The experience obviously gave Doreen a taste for launching things – she became an air traffic controller. (Courtesy Alexander Noble & Sons Ltd, Girvan)

Above:
40-footers
(1). *Wanderer*
(BA298)
kicking up the
spray. (Courtesy
Alexander
Noble & Sons
Ltd, Girvan)

Left: 40-footers
(2). *Hercules II*
(BA7) leaving
Girvan rather
more sedately.
(Courtesy
Alexander
Noble & Sons
Ltd, Girvan)

40-footers (3) – the next generation. *Emily J.* (E123). (Peter Drummond)

At sea (1). *Prospector* (TT25) towing. (Courtesy John M. Addison)

At sea (2). *Rosemary Ann* (BA279) hauling. (Courtesy John M. Addison)

At sea (3). *Marie* (BA211) lifting a catch aboard. (Courtesy Jeanie Maxwell)

At sea (4). *Pathfinder* (OB181) full of sprats. (Courtesy John M. Addison)

At sea (5). *Pathfinder* again, this time homeward bound when fishing as a prawn trawler. (Peter Drummond)

Seen from a distance (1). *Emily J.* (E123) makes her way out of Girvan for trials with a new main engine. (Peter Drummond)

Seen from a distance (2). *Comet*, retired from fishing but still active as a pleasure boat. (Courtesy M. Willis)

End of the *Integrity*. She is seen on the rocks at Portpatrick. (Courtesy William Ramsay)

End of the *Alison Mary*. As *Rose of Sharon V* (LH250) she is seen on the rocks at Seahouses. (Sam Henderson)

In for repair (1). *Stormdrift* (BA187) on what is known as Nobles' back slip in the company of the then new *Jasper* (SY379). (Courtesy Alexander Noble & Sons Ltd, Girvan)

In for repair (2). Two contrasting lifeboats slipped for overhaul. (Sam Henderson)

In for repair (3). It's all action at the yard as another lifeboat is slipped for overhaul. The Fowey lifeboat has traveled a long way to get her maintenance done. (Sam Henderson)

Left: In for repair (4). The 73ft steel motor yacht *Taora* of Guernsey ascends the slip. (Sam Henderson)

Below: In for repair (5). Two more of Nobles' own boats slipped for overhaul – *Village Belle IV* (TT74) and *Islander* (BA316). (Sam Henderson)

APPENDIX 3

NON-FISHING VESSELS

Above: The yacht *Oronsay* of Clynder built by Nobles as *Tunnag.* (Courtesy Matt Pye)

Left: Spanish John. (Courtesy Alexander Noble & Sons Ltd, Girvan)

Gizzen Briggs.
(Courtesy
Alexander Noble
& Sons Ltd,
Girvan)

Bata A Bhradain.
(Courtesy
Alexander Noble
& Sons Ltd,
Girvan)

Cassandra.
(Courtesy
Alexander Noble
& Sons Ltd,
Girvan)

Catriona.
(Courtesy
Alexander
Noble & Sons
Ltd, Girvan)

*Margaret
Sinclair.* (Sam
Henderson)

Carol Anne.
(Courtesy
Alexander
Noble & Sons
Ltd, Girvan)

Centaur. (Courtesy Alexander Noble & Sons Ltd, Girvan)

Dun Ghallain. (Courtesy Alexander Noble & Sons Ltd, Girvan)

Lady Ann. (Courtesy Alexander Noble & Sons Ltd, Girvan)

Lady Gael.
(Courtesy
Alexander Noble
& Sons Ltd,
Girvan)

Lady Katie.
(Courtesy
Alexander Noble
& Sons Ltd,
Girvan)

Lady Sarah.
(Courtesy
Alexander Noble
& Sons Ltd,
Girvan)

Loch Voshmid.
(Courtesy
Alexander Noble
& Sons Ltd,
Girvan)

Maid of Ulva.
(Courtesy
Alexander Noble
& Sons Ltd,
Girvan)

Mauy. (Courtesy
Alexander Noble
& Sons Ltd,
Girvan)

Sea Harvester. (Courtesy Alexander Noble & Sons Ltd, Girvan)

Sea Lion. (Courtesy Alexander Noble & Sons Ltd, Girvan)

Sidewinder. (Courtesy Alexander Noble & Sons Ltd, Girvan)

Two mini tugs under construction. (Courtesy Alexander Noble & Sons Ltd, Girvan)

Sarah Ann. (Sam Henderson)

APPENDIX 4

FISHING BOATS BUILT BY ALEXANDER NOBLE & SONS LTD

Note: Names given in block capitals are the vessels' original names.

AJ BA844
ALIPED VIII BA155, PL80, N57
ALIPED IX BA234, PD334, *Rona II* PD334
ALISON MARY N308, *Investor* BK107, *Rose of Sharon V* LH250
ALLIANCE CN187, *Alliance II* WD134
Alliance II WD134 – see ALLIANCE CN187
ANNABELLE BA115, A333, LT308
AQUILA OB99, *Beulah II* OB99, *Wanderer II* CN142
Astral INS116 – see WANDERER II BA76
Be Faithful PD307, B10 – see FAITHFUL PD307
Bessamarie BA212, AH120 – see JANET LANG CN84
Beulah II OB99 – see AQUILA OB99
Border Lassie BH44 – see CATHERINE R. ARMSTRONG BH44
Boy Cameron II BA141, INS314 – see ISLESMAN SY433
BOY JAMES BA52, DO12, B8, CT72, B128
BOY KEN TT70, *Frey* OB248, CT137
Brighter Morn CN151 – see SEEKER CN49
BRITANNIA BA130
Britannia V FH121 – see L & T BRITANNIA V FH121
CALEDONIA TT17, *Threshlyn* PL98, N98
CALINA SY47
Carra Rose CN194, LN193 – see JESSIE CN194
CATHERINE R. ARMSTRONG BH44, *Border Lassie* BH44
Comet BF430 – see MAGDALENA CY203
CRYSTAL SEA OB104, BA104, CN314, *Crystal Sea II* CN314, N314
Crystal Sea II CN314, N314 – see CRYSTAL SEA OB104
DALRIADA TT77, UL167, *Daystar* AH67, *Girl Margaret II* RO60, N914
DAWN MAID CT99, BA249, *Spes Bona IV* BA107, *Dawn Maid* TN102
Daystar AH67 – see DALRIADA TT77
Delta Dawn III SY788 – see JOB NO. 89 BA788

DEVORGILLA BA67, LH217, *Harvester* PD98, *Good Hope* FR891, B900
ELIZABETH CAMPBELL CN186, B58, S0283, B179, PL56
EMILY J. E123
EXCELLENT III OB89, SY289
Fair Morn BA19, SY529 – see JASPER SY379
FAITHFUL PD307, *Be Faithful* PD307, B10
FENELLA ANN CT27
Freedom IV LH371 – see WANDERER II BA76
Frey OB248, CT137 – see BOY KEN TT70
Girl Margaret II RO60, N914 – see DALRIADA TT77
GIRL MAUREEN BA128, TT30, LH148, *Morning Star* ME106, OB426, *Girl Maureen* BA142
Good Hope FR891, B900 – see DEVORGILLA BA67
Harvester PD98 – see DEVORGILLA BA67
HERCULES II BA7, UL156, LK438
Huntress BA93 – see WESTERLEA OB93
INTEGRITY BA335
Investor BK107 – see ALISON MARY N308
ISLESMAN SY433, BA141, *Boy Cameron II* BA141, INS314, *Islander* BA316
Islander BA316 – see ISLESMAN SY433
JANET LANG CN84, *Bessamarie* BA212, AH120, *New Era* OB90, *Morina* WK196, KY58, *Lupin*
    BF231, FH139
JASMINE BA55, CN110
JASPER SY379, *Santa Maria III* CY38, *Fair Morn* BA19, SY529
JESSIE CN194, *Carra Rose* CN194, LN193, *Sundance* LT577
JOB NO 89 BA788, *Delta Dawn III* SY788
L & T BRITANNIA V FH121, *Britannia V* FH121
Lorraine WA6 – see SYRINEN WA6
Lupin BF231, FH139 – see JANET LANG CN84
MAGDALENA CY203, *Comet* BF430
MAGDALENE ANN CT33, SH33
Maid of Honour CN120, LH120 – see SAFFRON BA182
MARGARET STEPHEN BA251, *Star of Hope II* CN262, *Wild Rover* BW21, SD70
MARGARETS LH232
MARIE BA211
MARIGOLD BA16, OB32, PW73, *Marigold A* CO423
Marigold A CO423 – see MARIGOLD BA16
MAUREEN PATRICIA CT18, OB582, CT18, N264, CT76
MICHAEL J. CT 9, K926, CT93, B116, BM138, PL74, K390
MIZPAH BA11, BA12, N903
Morina WK196, KY58 – see JANET LANG CN84
Morning Star ME106, OB426 – see GIRL MAUREEN BA128
MOYALLON OB24
NEW DAWN BA19, LH39
New Era OB90 – see JANET LANG CN84
OCEAN GEM BA265
Ocean Harvest BH46 – see SEEKER CN49
PATHFINDER BA252, OB181
PROSPECTOR BA25, SH2, TT25, N1
Provider A BH7, AH27 – see ROSE OF SHARON M.N349

RADIANCE BA289, CN132, TT97, N497, PL12, OB6, LK101
RAMBLING ROSE N359, BCK21
RANGER BA290, INS30, SY37, *Ranger A* SY37
Ranger A SY37 – see RANGER BA290
Reaper BF396, FR17, WK87 – see SELINA II BA333
REBENA BELLE CT63, N313
Regina Maris CY105 – see SILVERY SEA OB156
Ribhinn Bhan SY371, PL89, B23 – see RIBHINN DONN SY371
RIBHINN DONN SY371, *Ribhinn Bhan* SY371, PL89, B23
RIBHINN DONN II SY141, B140
Rona II PD334 – see ALIPED IX BA234
ROSE OF SHARON M.N349, BH7, *Provider A* BH7, AH27
Rose of Sharon V LH250 – see ALISON MARY N308
ROSEMARY ANN BA279, B279
SAFFRON BA182, *Maid of Honour* CN120, LH120, *Saffron* LH120, *Utopia* B563
SAPPHIRE BA174, CN174, N64
Santa Maria III CY38 – see JASPER SY379
SEASCAN WA16
SEEKER CN49, *Brighter Morn* CN151, *Seeker* CN151, *Sweet Promise* SS95,
Ocean Harvest BH46, *Seeker* CN694
SELINA II BA333, *Reaper* BF396, FR17, WK87
Sharon Rose SY190 – see SPINDRIFT BA220
Silver Dawn CN199, OB333 – see VILLAGE MAID SY63
SILVER CHORD BA62, *Stroma* BA62
SILVER QUEST BA302, DO76
SILVERY SEA OB156, CY105 *Regina Maris* CY105
SPES BONA BA17, BCK17, OB310
SPES BONA II BA107, *Spes Nova* CN77
Spes Bona IV BA107 – see DAWN MAID CT99, BA249
Spes Nova CN77 –see SPES BONA II BA107
SPINDRIFT BA220, Sharon Rose SY190
Star of Hope II CN262 – see MARGARET STEPHEN BA251
STJERNEN WA31
STORMDRIFT BA187, CN368
Stroma BA62 – see SILVER CHORD BA62
SUMMER MORN B78
Sundance LT577 – see JESSIE CN194
Sunrise LK76 – see WANDERER II BA76
Sweet Promise SS95 – see SEEKER CN49
SYRINEN WA6, *Lorraine* WA6, *Syrinen* WA6, BS2
Threshlyn PL98, N98 – see CALEDONIA TT17
TRUE TOKEN B600, CN298
Utopia B563 – see SAFFRON BA182
VALAURA BA256
VIGILANT SY28, UL55
VILLAGE BELLE IV TT74
VILLAGE MAID SY63, *Silver Dawn* CN199, OB333
VILLAGE MAID II TT25, OB154
WANDERER BA298, PD181, WK501, A279, CN79

WANDERER II BA76, *Freedom IV* LH371, *Sunrise* LK76, *Astral* INS116
Wanderer II CN142 – see AQUILA OB99
WESTERLEA OB93, *Huntress* BA93
Wild Rover BW21, SD70 – see MARGARET STEPHEN BA251

APPENDIX 5

NON-FISHING BOATS BUILT BY ALEXANDER NOBLE & SONS LTD

Year	No. Built	Name	Length	Yard Owner
1948	3	*Barkett*	17.68m	Commerce International
1952	14	*Accordance*	19.20m	Husbands Shipping, Southampton
1952	15	Unrecorded Motor Sailor	4.57m	Mr Lamont
1952	16	Two Rowing Dinghies	3.43m	
1953	17	Two Sailing Dinghies	3.05m	
1954	19	Yacht *Tunnag*	12.19m	Mr Findlay, Glasgow
1959	32	Pilot Boat *Cumbria*	10.67m	Trinity House, Workington
1981	81	*Susannah*	6.10m	Mr Kerrison, Colchester
1985	82	*Kingfisher II*	11.60m	Mr Medina, Ayr
1989	87	*Bata A Bhradain*	12.50m	Camus Mhor, Fish Farms, Onich
1990	88	*Cassandra*	14.00m	Fort William B.P. Nutrition, Lismore, Oban
1990	90	*Catriona*	14.00m	Mull Salmon Ltd, S te near Ulva
1990	91	*Lady Ann*	13.00m	Joseph Johnston & Sons Ltd, Scourie
1991	92	*Grace*	8.00m	Joseph Johnston & Sons Ltd, Scourie
1991	93	*Pamela*	8.00m	Joseph Johnston & Sons Ltd, Scourie
1991	94	*Kimberley*	8.00m	Joseph Johnston & Sons Ltd, Scourie
1992	95	*Maid of Bute*	14.00m	Kyle's of Bute, Salmon, Tighnabruaich
1992	96	*Lady Jean*	15.8m	Stirling Aquatic, Nr. Oban
1993	97	*Maid of Ulva*	15.8m	Kerrera Fisheries, Oban
1994	98	*Lady Sarah*	15.8m	Joseph Johnston, Scourie
1994	99	*Lady Jennifer*	15.8m	Lighthouse of Scotland
1994	100	*Sea Lion*	15.8m	Ardvaar Salmon
1995	101	*Lady Gael*	15.8m	Strathaird Farms, Skye
1995	102	*Ribhinn Loch Rog*	12.00m	Marine Harvest, McConnell

1996	103	Sheilavaig	12.00m	Marine Harvest, McConnell
1996	104	Mini tug		Gulf Offshore
1996	105	Mini tug		Gulf Offshore
1996	106	Mini tug		Gulf Offshore
1996	107	Loch Voshmid	15.30m	Marine Harvest, McConnell
1997	108	Sea Harvester	15.40m	Marine Harvest, McConnell
1997	109	Sophie Ann	15.80m	Lighthouse of Scotland
1997	110	Dun Ghallain	15.80m	Marine Harvest, McConnell
1998	111	Lady Inger	12.00m	Lighthouse of Scotland
1998	112	Stolt Iasg	15.30m	Stolt Sea Farm Ltd
1998	113	Stolt Reece	15.30m	Stolt Sea Farm Ltd
1999	114	Lady Mia	16.90m	Lighthouse of Scotland
1999	115	Carol Anne	16.2m	Mr David Pollard, Kilmore, Argyll
2000	116	Ashleanne	12.9m	Hydro Seafoods, GSP
2000	117	Salarus	12.9m	Hydro Seafoods GSP
2000	118	Lady Katie	9.5m	Lighthouse of Scotland
2000	119	Sally Ruth	9.5m	Lighthouse of Scotland
2000	120	Melissa	16.9m	Lighthouse of Scotland
2001	121	Kerry	12.9m	Lighthouse of Scotland
2001	122	Mauy	14.9m	Aquascot Group Ltd
2001	123	Sidewinder	8.5m	Myti Mussels
2002	124	Centaur	13.00m	Demlane Ltd
2002	125	Spanish John II	19.00m	Milligan Transport Ltd
2003	126	Adsa III	15.00m	Alevines y Doradas SA, Spain
2003	127	Unnamed	7.5m	
2004	128	Gizzen Briggs	13.00m	Highland Fresh Mussels
2006	131	Margaret Sinclair	21m	Inverlussa Shellfish Co. Ltd
2008	132	Lady Heather		Loch Duart Ltd
2009	133	Sarah Ann	19.5m	Lakeland Marine Farms

Note:
(1) The pilot boat Cumbria was for a time registered as WA12 and used for fishing. She has now been decommissioned.
(2) Kingfisher was registered as BA149 to create the option of use as a fishing vessel but was instead used as a sea angling boat.

Other titles published by The History Press

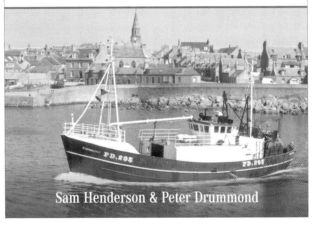

Fishing Boats of Campeltown Shipyard
Sam Henderson & Peter Drummond

Today the empty buildings which once comprised Campeltown Shipyard betray no trace of the hive of activity which once existed there and produced some of the finest fishing vessels ever built in Scotland. Nontheless with surviving boats still turning in impressive performance, the fishing industry will long remember the fishing boats of Campeltown Shipyard.

978 0 7524 4765 0

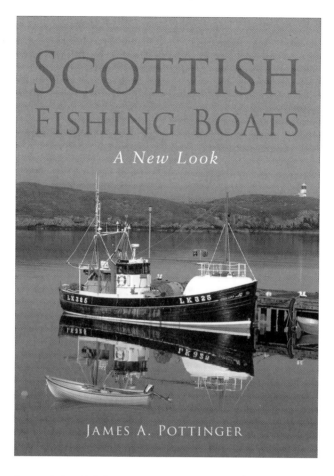